PEOPLE OF SCILLY

By the same author
Falkland People

PEOPLE OF SCILLY

ANGELA WIGGLESWORTH

Foreword by Leslie Thomas

ALAN SUTTON PUBLISHING LIMITED

First published in the United Kingdom in 1994
Alan Sutton Publishing Ltd · Phoenix Mill · Far Thrupp · Stroud · Gloucestershire

First published in the United States of America in 1994
Alan Sutton Publishing Inc · 83 Washington Street · Dover NH 03820

Reprinted 1994

British Library Cataloguing in Publication Data
A catalogue record for this book is available from the British Library

ISBN 0-7509-0663-4

Library of Congress Cataloging in Publication Data applied for

Cover illustrations: front: St Martin's from the air (*by kind permission of the Isles of Scilly Tourist Board*); *insets*: Louise Walder, John Hicks; *back*: cottage on St Martin's.

Typeset in 10/13 pt Times.
Typesetting and origination by
Alan Sutton Publishing Limited.
Printed in Great Britain by
Redwood Books, Trowbridge.

CONTENTS

ACKNOWLEDGEMENTS

I would like to thank Clive Mumford for checking the manuscript, and Mike Nelham, Keith Low, Marian Bennett and Wendy Hick for reading the sections on Tresco, St Martin's, Bryher and St Agnes. I'd also like to thank Kathy Stedeford, David Haskins, Steve Watt and Mark Wigglesworth who helped in other practical ways.

I'm very grateful to The Isles of Scilly Skybus and National Express Ltd, for their assistance with transport; to the Queen's Hotel in Penzance for their hospitality; and to Pat and Gerry Twynham of Trevean Guest House, St Mary's, for their help and encouragement.

All photographs are by Angela Wigglesworth with the exception of the following from Frank Gibson (pp. 28, 44, 51, 64, 66, 67, 73, 132, 134, 135, 136, 137); Kevin Tobyn-Duggan (pp. 110, 115); Mark Groves (p. 60).

Finally, I would like to express my appreciation to all the people of Scilly who gave me their time without which this book would not have been possible, and to the many others I would like to have included if only the book could have been twice the size.

FOREWORD

When I first went to the Isles of Scilly in the early 1950s they were unknown to many people in Britain. I recall sending a postcard to someone who later asked me how I had enjoyed visiting 'Sicily'.

In those days you either travelled in one of the earlier generation *Scillonians* or took the fairly exciting flight from the grass runway at St Just, on the end of Cornwall, in a De Haviland Dragonfly – the only aeroplane, so I have heard, ever to be retired through having woodworm in the airframe!

The isolation of the islands has made for a singular set of people. When I first arrived there was much grumbling in The Mermaid about the possible introduction of Income Tax. But like most other vicissitudes, the islanders survived it.

On that first visit I could hardly believe how tranquil the place was. Walking along the harbour at Hugh Town on St Mary's on a spring morning I felt the peace of the islands – the shining sea, the sky full of gulls, the boats and the little town itself lost in calmness.

A view of St Mary's, across the harbour

Each of the islanders in this book has had their life and experience shaped by the smallness of the land and the vastness of the sea. They live surprisingly ordinary lives considering their romantic home but underlying their testimony you can almost hear the running of the tides and the sound of the maritime wind. On an island 2½ miles by 1¾, Eric Woodcock, the St Mary's bus driver, must travel one of the world's shortest routes. But the island bus has always been a lively place for conversation, however brief. Clive Mumford's family I have known for a long time. Their newspaper shop is one of the landmarks of Hugh Town. Although he is additionally a journalist, surely a unique combination, he is an islander first and with him a confidence is a confidence. Rodney Ward, one of the oldest islanders, remembers days as far gone as those shown in the now sepia photographs taken by the Gibson family.

From Lady Wilson, the wife of Lord Wilson, to Keith Low, the fisherman-crofter of St Martin's, these people speak of their islands with loyalty and affection but without false sentiment. Scilly is where they live and work.

Angela Wigglesworth has been able to get them to talk about themselves, shy though some of them are, and has succeeded in gently getting below the top layer of their lives. The Scillonians welcomed her into their homes and spoke of their thoughts, ambitions and memories. She has respected what she has been told and the result is a unique and most readable social document about an outpost of our country.

Leslie Thomas
1994

BRIEF HISTORY

AD 400 to 1100. Christian hermits lived on some of the islands.

800–1570. Scilly used as a base for pirates.

994. The Viking Olaf Tryggvesson, King of Norway, came to Scilly with nearly 100 ships, was converted to Christianity, and subsequently introduced it to Norway and Iceland.

1114. Henry I granted Tresco and neighbouring islands to the Abbey of Tavistock, and a Benedictine priory was established on Tresco.

1248. Dreux de Barrentine was sent by Henry III to be Governor of the Isles.

1306. Scilly leased at a yearly rent of 6s 8d (33p) or 300 puffins.

1337. The Isles of Scilly were included in the Duchy of Cornwall and given to the Black Prince.

1484. Value of Scilly in peacetime, 40s; in war, nothing.

1539. The monastery of Tavistock was dissolved.

1571. Queen Elizabeth I leased the islands to Francis Godolphin.

1593–4. Star Castle was built on the Hugh to prevent the islands being used as a base by Spain, at war with England until 1604.

1623. Prince Charles, later Charles II, stayed on St Mary's for four days.

1637–81. Star Castle used as a prison.

1646. Prince Charles took refuge for six weeks at Star Castle. He escaped to Jersey and the Isles of Scilly surrendered to Parliament.

1648–51. Rebellion of Scilly. In the hands of Royalists under Sir John Grenville, privateers plundered passing ships.

1651. The Dutch, incensed by the piracy of the Scilly rebels, declared war on the islands and sent a fleet of twelve men-of-war. They were prevented from attacking by the arrival of the English fleet also intent on subduing the Royalist rebels. In May Sir John Grenville surrendered and Scilly became the last Royalist stronghold in England to do so.

1684. Kelp-ash – obtained by burning seaweed and of use to glass makers, soap manufacturers and bleachers – began to be made in Scilly.

1707. Four ships of the fleet under the command of Sir Cloudesley Shovell (*Association*, *Eagle*, *Romney*, *Firebrand*) were wrecked on the Western Rocks and over 1,600 men were lost.

1742–1834. There was much poverty and the islanders relied on fishing, kelp-making and smuggling.

1743. John Wesley visited Scilly.

1744. The Hugh was surrounded by fortifications and bastions and the Garrison gateway dates from this time.

1810. Trinity House took over pilotage in Scilly, formerly licensed by the Council of Twelve. (In 1810 there were seventy-six licensed pilots; in 1993 there are two.)

1831. The Duke of Leeds (Godolphin) did not renew the lease; Scilly reverted to the Duchy of Cornwall.

1834. Augustus Smith, a Hertfordshire squire, obtained the lease of the islands from the Crown and became Lord Proprietor. He built a house (Tresco Abbey), laid out the Abbey gardens, built schools and introduced compulsory education long before it existed on the mainland. Compulsory meant paying 1*d* a day to attend, 2*d* for non-attendance.

1835–71. Shipbuilding became an important industry and at one time there were five yards on St Mary's. The industry flourished until iron vessels replaced wooden ones.

1849. First Bishop lighthouse under construction.

1855. Augustus Smith ordered the evacuation of Samson, possibly because the inhabitants were too old to man the fishing boats and support themselves.

1858. Penzance to Scilly steam ferry began. Bishop Rock lighthouse rebuilt – the first was destroyed in an 1850 gale before it was completed.

1859. Great Western Railway extended to Penzance and excursion trips to Scilly began. Especially popular were Augustus Smith's sub-tropical gardens on Tresco.

1869. Telegraph company formed by Scillonians to lay the first cable to the mainland.

1872 Augustus Smith died and was succeeded by his nephew, Lieut. T. Smith-Dorrien who changed the name to Smith-Dorrien Smith.

1900–4. Gun emplacements and forts were built on the Hugh but abandoned after a quarter of a million pounds had been spent on a plan to make the islands a naval base.

1914–18. A seaplane base of the 34th Royal Navy Air squadron was established on St Mary's and from 1917 on Tresco.

1918. Major A.A. Dorrien Smith DSO succeeded his father, Lieut. T. Dorrien Smith.

1920. Lease of all inhabited islands, except Tresco, relinquished. The Duchy of Cornwall began direct administration of St Mary's (except Hugh Town), St Martin's, St Agnes and Bryher.

1925. The first issue of *The Scillonian*, then a quarterly now a biannual magazine, was published.

1937. First scheduled air service of twin-engined De Havilland Dragon biplanes from St Just to St Mary's, using the golf course as a landing-strip. The present airport opened in 1939.

1939–45. Islands used as a base in the war against hostile submarines, one of which was bombed and sunk after striking the Western Rocks, and another claimed by the Wolf Rock. A flight of Hurricane fighter aircraft and two air-sea rescue launches were stationed at St Mary's. The islands received much machine-gun fire and about two hundred bombs.

1949. The Duchy of Cornwall offered the freehold of its properties in Hugh Town to sitting tenants. Most took up the offer.

1954. Income tax introduced to Scilly for the first time.

1955. Major A.A. Dorrien Smith died and was succeeded to the lease of Tresco by his son, Lt.-Com. T.M. Dorrien Smith RN (retired).

1964. Biplanes replaced by helicopters, the first helicopter service to be operated by British European Airways.

1966. A new secondary school was opened on St Mary's.

1971. Motor taxation introduced to Scilly for the first time.

1973. Robert Dorrien Smith succeeded to the lease of Tresco.

1977. The ferry *Scillonian III* came into service.

1983. Tresco heliport opened.

1985. The inhabited off-islands received mains electricity linked to St Mary's by undersea cable.

1987. Skybus service began with flights from Land's End aerodrome at St Just to St Mary's. The Duchy of Cornwall leased the uninhabited islands and untenanted land for a hundred years at a peppercorn rent, to the newly formed Isles of Scilly Environmental Trust.

1989. Mainland electricity came to Scilly by means of a 36 mile undersea cable – the longest in Britain. The freight ship *Gri Maritha* came into service; also the *Busant*, *Northolm* and *Fair Islander*.

1991. Airport runway extended to enable larger aircraft to land.

1992. Desalination water plant installed.

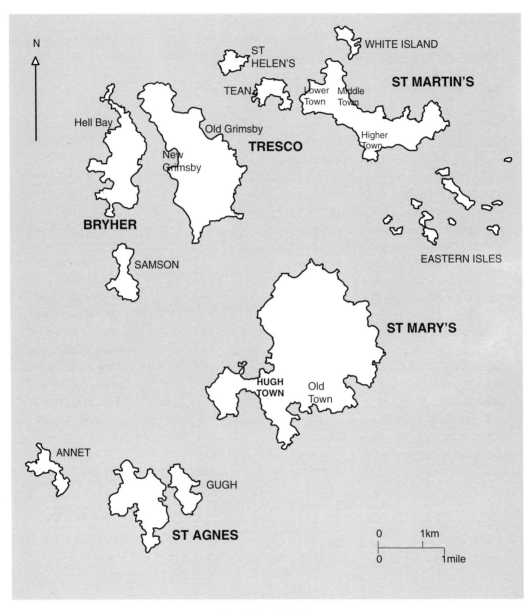

N

WHITE ISLAND

ST
HELEN'S

TEAN

ST MARTIN'S

Lower
Town

Middle
Town

Old Grimsby

TRESCO

Higher
Town

Hell Bay

New
Grimsby

BRYHER

SAMSON

EASTERN ISLES

ST MARY'S

HUGH
TOWN

Old
Town

ANNET

GUGH

ST AGNES

0		1km
0		1mile

The Isles of Scilly

INTRODUCTION

The Isles of Scilly are a group of about fifty-four tiny islands, 11 miles from east to west, 5 from north to south, 28 miles off the south-west tip of Land's End, and part of the Duchy of Cornwall since 1337. They lie clustered together in an unpolluted blue sea, with white sandy beaches, fields of daffodils flowering in December, wild orchids in the hedgerows in summer. Huge rocks hewn into primeval shapes jut from the sea where seals and dolphins swim, and in the cottage gardens dazzlingly bright mesembryanthemums cover low grey stone walls in early summer and blue-flowered echium trees stand like sentinels. October brings bird-watchers from all over the country who come to see rare species blown in from Siberia or North America.

Some think the islands are the legendary lost Land of Lyonesse. They were certainly the hilltops of a much larger land area, and when the tide goes out today it is possible to walk between some of them. Only five are inhabited: St Mary's, the largest, is 2½ miles by 1¾ and home to 1,600 of the islands' 2,000 population. With its shops, restaurants, pubs, cafés, hotels and guest-houses, it has a bustle about it that is noticeably absent from the other islands. Tresco has sub-tropical gardens; St Martin's perhaps the finest beaches; on St Agnes you can hunt for beads buried in the sand from a seventeenth-century wreck; on Bryher, waves crash spectacularly on to the gigantic rocks of Hell Bay, sending spray hundreds of feet into the air. The uninhabited islands are home to puffins, gannets and the Atlantic Grey seals and most are open to the public though some are closed for conservation purposes during certain months.

There is virtually no crime on Scilly. The two policemen know almost everyone by their first name, and children have a freedom to wander without fear, something undreamt of on the mainland today. Magistrates meet once a month, but there is often nothing to discuss other than applications for licence extensions. It's a classless society where a dustman can (and has) played golf with a prime minister, and there are no party politics in the Isles of Scilly Council, which is of parish proportions, but with County Council powers.

There are few private cars except on St Mary's, no traffic lights, no MOTs, Sunday papers arrive on Monday, and tides rather than time control events. There is a story about one off-island small general store selling newspapers. 'Could I have *The Times*,' asked a visitor. 'Today's or yesterday's?' asked the manager. 'Today's,' replied the customer. 'Well, then,' said the manager, 'you'll have to come tomorrow.'

The bus on St Mary's stops where you want it, the airport bus drops you at your destination, and no one locks their front doors or their cars. It's easy to see why the islands are called The Fortunate Isles.

'If you get hooked on Scilly, you are hooked for life, it's addictive,' one visitor told me. But Scilly, as everywhere else, has its problems. Flower farmers are concerned about the fate of their once prosperous industry; those involved in tourism – and almost everyone is to some degree – are anxious about the falling number of visitors and the cost of travel to the islands. Isles of Scilly councillors and the Duchy of Cornwall Land Steward struggle with the problem of wanting to provide houses for young Scillonian-born people who want to live and work here, but have to impose restrictions on development in order not to destroy the beauty of the landscape that visitors come to see.

It's hard to believe there are only 28 miles between Scilly and the mainland. Scillonians don't even feel Cornish, let alone English. As Steve Watt, the Tourism Officer and a Scillonian himself, told me, 'We regard England as a small island, east-north-east of Scilly. We're not really Cornish, though if it came to a fight and it was Cornwall versus the rest, we know which side we'd be on. We're a separate kingdom altogether. We're Scillonians.'

And the boatman, John Hicks, told me, 'I'll feel Cornish when a Cornishman feels English. I'm a Scillonian.'

But what makes a Scillonian? It's not enough to be born on Scilly to call yourself one. In fact, there are varying interpretations of the right to do so, but the general consensus seems to be that you need three generations of islanders on both sides of the family behind you.

The late Ron Perry, who took bus tours round St Mary's and was famous for his laconic, humorous commentaries, once gave me a description of Scilly which still seems to fit: 'Rocks and sand and barren land, a church without a steeple. Houses made of ship-wrecked wood, full of happy people.'

This book is about these people. Not all Scillonians, but people who live and work on the islands and make them what they are today.

ST MARY'S

St Mary's is the largest of the islands, 2½ miles by 1¾, with 9 miles of coastline, and a population of 1,600. Hugh Town, the islands' only town, straddling a narrow sandy isthmus, has a variety of small shops, pubs, hotels, guest-houses, restaurants, churches, a hospital, a post office, two banks, a museum and two hairdressers. The ferry to the mainland and pleasure boats operate from the quay, and the Isles of Scilly Steamship Company and British Airways both have offices in the main street. Star Castle, built in 1593 as a garrison and now a hotel, stands high over the town.

There are no names on the streets, which makes finding them slightly difficult for visitors but, I was told, this is how they, the visitors, like it. There are more signposts now than there used to be, but the most popular boards are those showing which boat is going to which island and when, though cheerful boatmen from the St Mary's Boatmen Association will already have made a breakfast-time call to hotels and guest-houses to discuss the day's weather and likely sailings.

The island has ancient monuments, Civil War castles, great rock formations at Peninnis Head, and hides for bird-watchers. There are fine sandy beaches, woodland and coastal walks, a nine hole golf-course, and flowers everywhere at almost any time of the year.

THE BUS DRIVER

Sixty-eight-year-old Eric Woodcock's ancestors were among the last to leave the now uninhabited island of Samson last century. He comes from a farming family and was a farmer himself until 1971 when he became a bus driver. Now, in partnership with his nephew, Derek Woodcock, he drives the twenty-six seater country bus, and Derek looks after the '007' – the airport bus for helicopter passengers.

This is a service bus. We drop you off anywhere you want to go and pick you up anywhere. There are no recognized stops. I shout out the names of places where people normally go and if they want to get off, they get off. If someone on the road puts their hand up, I stop and they jump on. There's a flat fare of 80p wherever you go and you pay as you leave. People are very surprised when they say to me, 'Can you change a £10 note?' and I say, 'No, I can't, pay me when you come back.' They're not accustomed to anything like that. But I've never been diddled.

The bus only runs from Easter to the end of October and the locals use it quite a lot for shopping. I publish a timetable. In fact I have two. Now, in May, I'm on the short one, but from next Bank Holiday to September, I'll be on the longer one which means more trips and a later one at night. At the moment it's 10 p.m., but it will be 10.45 p.m. then.

In October we get the bird-watchers and they bring an awful lot of money to the island. There can be five hundred at a time. You might be sat here empty and all of a sudden there's a rare bird seen and there's an invasion. They all pile on – I've had seventy aboard. How they get on, I don't know and even if they only go half a mile, they still pay. They'd pay anything to get there, they're so keen on their hobby. There was a period when we had a lot causing trouble, knocking down hedges, going through people's fields leaving gates open, but nowadays you get a totally different class of person. A lot of professional people, mostly men, but funnily enough there's more ladies coming nowadays. At one time it was all men, and if you saw a lady bird-watcher you thought 'Good God, what's this?'

THE POLICE SERGEANT

I'm very much a community-orientated person and that was really what was needed here. Someone who would join in, get out on the street, talk to people, act as a catalyst. There's an expression we use which is 'policing by consent'. The way I read this is you get the police force you deserve. If people want to get drunk, make a lot of noise and drive round on poor tyres, then they'll need and get a strong police presence. If you take a policeman's advice ('your tyres aren't looking very good, get them done by next Tuesday') then you'll get a police force that will police that way. So far here, everyone's agreed with me. I don't have to stick parking tickets on cars, I just say, 'Now look, during the summer I don't want cars parked in the High Street.' Last week I issued the first parking ticket on Scilly, though I didn't realize it, and it hit the national news. The population had doubled that weekend for the World Gig Championships and gig rowers are known for their drinking and singing as much as rowing. Fifteen hundred people came to the island, which almost doubled its population and quadrupled the consumption of alcohol, yet there wasn't a single voice raised in anger, nothing was stolen and no offences committed. That's what the press should be putting out about Scilly: that we have this unique atmosphere which affects people when they arrive, no matter how bad they are.

There are 9 miles of A-class roads on St Mary's, no traffic lights, zebra crossings, or roundabouts and people have the opportunity to take a driving test twice a year. We've had to tighten up a bit on the condition of motor vehicles – we don't have MOT tests and a lot of the vehicles were getting to be criminally dangerous. The Road Traffic Act now applies to St Mary's, but not the off-islands where you could see a twelve-year-old driving a 1,200 cc motor cycle with no crash helmet, no tax, no licence, no MOT, no insurance, because it's private land owned by the Duchy.

We did have a drink–driving campaign just before Christmas – we were a bit concerned that was getting lax as

Alan Russell, forty-nine, is Head of the Island Police Force (which consists of two regular officers and two female Specials) and has an Open University Honours Degree in Educational Psychology. He is married to Tricia and they have two married daughters and one son. Over the past twelve years they have been foster parents to forty-nine children.

well. We're in the lucky position of knowing who owns which car and where they are, and we went to every single vehicle on the island, which is some six hundred, and put a leaflet inside telling the owners what we were going to do. We still use the old blow-in-the-bag breathalyser, and we took a few which were past their sell-by date, and asked people heading towards their cars, 'Are you going to drive? Well, just as a favour to yourself and to me, have a blow in this.' And the results surprised them. I then told them that if they drove their car they would be committing an offence. 'Thanks very much,' they said. 'I'm walking home and here's my keys. I'll collect them in the morning.' The nice thing about this is that people who don't listen to you, don't have any excuse.

It's like the faulty exhaust. I might tell you, 'Your exhaust is faulty and I want you to get it fixed.' And you say, 'OK, I'll go down the garage this afternoon and order one.' And then you come back and say, 'It won't be in till next Tuesday.' 'Right,' I say, 'next Wednesday I want you to come to the police station together with your vehicle and your new exhaust pipe on it.' They come up on Tuesday and the steamship hasn't come, or the helicopter has broken down, and say, 'I'm sorry, it hasn't arrived.' 'OK, fine,' I say, 'I'll give you another week.'

I think that's the island ethic. If you're fair with me, I'm fair with you and that's the way we try and work here. But this can be a drawback in that they rely on you to tell them. 'My tyre must be alright,' they think, 'because Sergeant Russell hasn't said it isn't.'

I think we've got the trust of the adult population – we know we have the juniors'. We go to the playschool and Tresco are bringing their kids to visit the station next month. I run the junior rugby team which is something new here, and I've got about forty kids coming up on a Sunday morning for practice. There's none of this 'Sir', touch your forelock. I'm the guy who blows the whistle and teaches them rugby.

We have two cells, one to store the police bicycle and Christmas lights, the other in case we need it. We had a drunk in eight months ago but we can only keep anyone in custody for six hours and then they have to go to the mainland. So if you arrest someone at 3 p.m., you have to release him at 9 p.m. that night. The magistrates court is scheduled for once a month, but is cancelled if there's no business, as happened three times last year, though the Joint Police Committee (a group of magistrates and councillors who license applications for extensions) meet once every two months.

I can say quite categorically there is no problem with drugs on the islands but I'd be a very foolish person if I said there there were no drugs on the island. I'm sure social drug-taking takes place but we don't have people into heavy drugs. Parents on the island are very aware of the symptoms to look for.

The only time we note a crime is when we catch someone doing something and a complaint is made. We had a guy who broke a window in a drunken stupor and we begged the owners of the house to make a complaint so we could put the guy before a court to get some help with his alcoholism. But they said, 'Oh poor chap' and didn't want to do anything about it. There's no street fighting, it's mostly thefts from boats and that's not necessarily by people from this country.

I retire in three and a half years' time and I'm dreading going back to the mainland. The whole world should be looking at Scilly and saying this is how we want to be, how we should be, because it does work. I publish my home telephone number, I don't lock my doors, my personal car is round the corner, my keys are in it. If I look out the window and see my van's gone, I say someone's borrowed it. I do miss being able to go to a shop to buy a specific thing, and not having to wait seven weeks for the man to mend my washing machine. The police pay for four trips away and we need them. But two days later I want to come back.

In Hayle, my home town on the mainland, I'm Mr Russell, a policeman from Penzance. Here you are a policeman twenty-four hours a day whether you're in uniform or out of it and you just have to accept that. I'm Sergeant Russell, though most of the time it's Alan.

THE PAPER SHOP OWNER AND JOURNALIST

Clive Mumford, fifty-five, has several generations of Scillonians on his father's side of the family. He worked on regional newspapers until, in 1984, he decided to return to Scilly to run the family Paper Shop. He is now a local councillor, edits *The Scillonian* magazine and is island correspondent for *The Cornishman*. He also freelances for *West Country* and national papers, radio and TV. He is married to Avril with three grown-up daughters by his first wife.

The family has had The Paper Shop for nearly a hundred years – it's the oldest business on Scilly and was started by my grandparents. It has remained the same old Paper Shop, with a few refinements, but I don't want too many. Everything revolves around the receipt of newspapers from the helicopter and they come in around 9.30 a.m. If there's fog, they come by the steamer about lunch-time. We get no papers on a Sunday – they arrive on a Monday because there's no Sunday transport. One customer buys his on a Monday, sticks it in a wardrobe unread for a week, and then produces it with a big flourish with his boiled egg the following Sunday. He doesn't worry too much if it's a week old.

One day we didn't get enough papers to go round and I had to ration visitors but let the locals have what they always had. One military gentleman, having seen four go to the lifeboat cox, asked for the *Observer* and *Sunday Times*. I said I was terribly sorry but he could only have one. He blustered that he'd been all round the world and never found such discrimination. When he got back home to Esher, he said, he'd tell his MP friend about the incident. Just at that moment, Harold Wilson, then Prime Minister, walked in. I said to the customer, 'Look, Sir, don't mess around with backbench MPs, why not go right to the top and solve this predicament now?' Then I said to Harold Wilson, 'Mr Wilson, you haven't got a second, have you?' Mr Wilson turned round and said, 'Hello, Clive.' The chap looked at him and shot out of the door. I've never seen anyone move so fast.

It's the scale of Scilly that sells a newspaper story because when you compare it with the mainland it's absurd. And therein lies the problem. I have to be very cautious that I'm not making fun of someone or making Scilly look stupid, because I love Scilly. It's a thin line and many times I've sat on a good story and not used it when I could have made quite a lot of money from it. People phone up and say, 'Will you interview so and so?' And I say, 'I can't.'

And they say, 'Are you a journalist?' And I say, 'Well I am, but not to that extent.' And of course they can't understand it, but I have to live here. On the other hand, some things can seem enormously important here and are of no consequence whatsoever on the mainland.

It's important to get away occasionally, not only to recharge the batteries and see there's another world out there, but to reinforce your views that you do live in a special place. It's a caring, small community with very little crime. They're beautiful islands, and anyone who does his or her best, regardless of his status, will be fully accepted and have a wonderful life. This is the delight of Scilly. There has been an acceleration in recent years of more mainland people coming to live here. When my father was chairman of the post-war Council, there were twenty-five councillors from all the islands put together, and only one mainland-born person. Now I think there are only six born Scillonians out of twenty-one. But it's invigorating to have new blood coming in.

Being on the local Council myself can make reporting meetings quite awkward sometimes. If you ask certain questions, they think you're doing so to get an answer for a good story. And you can't get the quotes you would normally get if you're actually participating in a debate. But I go and listen to committees which I'm not on, and get a full story there. It's a very testing job because Scilly has a lot of problems and much of the work is trying to shape the Scilly you want, to make sure what you value is not changed. We've got the powers of a County Council and it's a hell of a responsibility because if things go wrong, there's always the fear people will say we can't handle our own affairs, and we'll be incorporated with Cornwall and just be a crumb on the toe.

THE BUTCHER

Supermarkets were losing what I became a butcher for, which was talking to customers. That's what I enjoy about it here. Woodcock & Mumford has been going for 150 years but now it's just the Mumfords who run it and my

John Young, fifty-three, was a butcher with Sainsbury's in Coventry before coming to Scilly in 1970 to work for Woodcock & Mumford. He is Chairman of St Mary's Football Club.

7

boss is Mr Dudley Mumford. There's three of us in the shop all the year round, Dudley, myself and Trevor; we call him the young lad, but he's twenty-five now and has been here since he was seventeen. In summer, we have a delicatessen as well and sell up to fifty different sorts of cheese.

One of the things I enjoy is when a local girl comes in, she's having a dinner party in a fortnight's time and she's looked at her recipe book. She tells me she wants so and so on a particular day. Then you look at the recipe and say, 'Well, what are you doing with it?' And she says 'so and so'. And I say I think I could find a cut of meat that will do exactly the same job and save her money. She says, 'Well, you find what you think is the most appropriate thing.' She's guided by me and the nice thing is when she comes back after the party and says 'thank you very much, it was lovely'. A lot of cookery books tell you the most expensive things to use, but in the butchery line you can always find something just that little bit cheaper. There's nothing like this in a supermarket.

There are a lot more vegetarians now than there ever has been, over the last six or eight years. In fact, we sell quite a bit of vegetarian stuff in the shop. You have to move with the times and meat consumption these last few years has gone down a lot. But people still come in on a Saturday and want to spend £5 on a Sunday joint. They were spending that five years ago. I always say it's the only thing in the housewife's shopping basket where she can tell you how much she wants to spend. Buy a loaf of bread in a supermarket and she has to pay the recommended price. When she goes to the butcher's, she still says she wants £5 worth of meat, though no way are they getting so much.

A few years ago John Young hit the headlines in the national and international press when he was photographed watching a football match on St Mary's, in a portable cabin he'd made himself.

I'd been going up to watch football for many years and in the winter, with the wind blowing and the rain, you get freezing cold and drenched. One year, the St Mary's

Football Club invited the Supporters Club to a dinner and I was the only supporter. I sat there and they said, 'You've got to get up on behalf of the Supporters Club and say something.' I thought, what could I talk about? Well, one of the things I said was, 'Is it possible for you to find a proper seat for me to keep the rain out before next season?' and they just laughed.

Nothing happened and round about November I decided to make a little hut for myself. On the Sunday after I'd done it, I borrowed the van from the shop, drove up to the playing field, took out the hut, walked along the side of the pitch, set it down and that was it. The game came to a complete halt because they wondered what the hell was going on. I've had it ever since and it's gone through two seasons now. It's very light and I've put plastic in to make a window. The top is blue, the back is yellow, and there's a seat inside – it's only me sitting on it that stops the hut being blown away. I sit there and other people come up and say, 'Gosh, it's cold up here, John, isn't it?' and I say, 'No, I'm perfectly alright, it's lovely and warm in here.' And you wouldn't believe it, but since I built it, we haven't had a real heavy rainstorm and that's a record, I do know.

THE FLOWER BREEDER AND STEAMSHIP COMPANY PRESIDENT

It was my grandfather William Barnes who was one of three gentlemen who, in 1867, sent the first flowers from these islands to the mainland in an old-fashioned hat box. He and Mr Trevellick were in a garden one day and one of them said to the other, 'You know, if people in London could see these flowers they'd give us money for them.' So they hit on the idea of filling the hat box and sent them through the post. They got 7s 6d and that was real money in those days. So they thought they'd try another bigger box and this time they got £1. Well, they felt they ought to tell the landlord, one of the Dorrien Smiths from Tresco, which

Rodney Ward, eighty-nine, was born on St Mary's and began breeding daffodils when he left school. A former chairman of the Isles of Scilly Steamship Company, he retired in 1990, and became its first president. A former councillor and skipper of the cricket and football teams, he is married to Marianne. They have six grandchildren and twelve great-grandchildren.

they did and he went all over the world getting stocks of daffodil bulbs and planting them on the island. And that's really how the flower industry started.

In those days, it was the early bird that caught the worm, there were no artificial ways of bringing the flowers on, or making them later. The earliest of all yellow trumpets was called *Magnificence* and it's still growing. I thought I'd try and get something earlier by cross-pollinating and I selected three of my seedlings, *Fantee* and *Mando*, named after wrecks, and *Sanilly*, one of the Eastern Islands. My son later sold 5 cwt of *Mando* to a firm on the mainland and now this firm is cutting out everything in the yellow trumpet line but that.

I used to grow 20 acres of daffodils on our 33 acre farm, breeding over a hundred varieties, but didn't register them all. One famous one I raised was *Suhali*, named after Knox Johnston's yacht. Another was *Marjorie Treveal*, named after the secretary's wife at one of the Cornish shows. I was numbering my exhibits and this lady said to me, 'What do you mean, "seedling number . . ."?' and I said, 'That means I haven't named it yet, but what's your name?' And she said 'Marjorie', so I called that one after her for a joke. But her husband, he got up on the stage with the loudspeaker and roared through the hall that I'd just named a flower after his wife, so I had to register it then. I wasn't allowed to use my wife's name. She said, 'Don't you call one after me.'

The Steamship Company: When the First World War was finished there was only a trawler service to the mainland. One day the commander told Father they'd be pulling out in six months. So Father called a meeting of the islanders and they decided to start a fund with 5*s* shares. Father was fortunate to have a brother at the Admiralty who wrote and told him there was a boat for disposal called *The Argos* and that they wanted £15,000 for it. All the islanders could raise was £8,000, so my uncle, who was a very gifted speaker, told the Admiralty about these poor islanders, and had the Lords almost in tears. In the end they said that if the islanders couldn't raise any more money, they must have the boat for £8,000, and they did. The Steamship Company was founded in the same year, 1919, and in 1925 the first *Scillonian* was built. My father, as chairman, had never taken a salary, but I said I wasn't in a position to do the work for nothing – I'd have to get another man on the farm to take my place. They said, 'How much would that be?' and I said '£5', and so I managed that company for four or five years for £5 a week and was the only one who didn't ask for a rise, and the only one who didn't get one!

THE BOATMAN

Until the Boatmen's Association was formed, all the boats in St Mary's were independent. But as business grew, there was a lot of rivalry and touting and it was really spoiling Scilly for what it is – a fairly relaxed and friendly place. I think it was Mr Henry H.A. Thomas, Managing Director of the Steamship Company at the time, who said to my father, 'Look, why don't we try and knock all this in-fighting on the head and see if we can't work together?' and that sowed the seeds for the St Mary's Boatmen's Association, which works very well. There are ten boats now – all individually owned and maintained, and we have a rota system for daily trips. Every morning, boatmen come round to your breakfast table at the guest-houses and hotels and tell visitors where they can go that day. That doesn't happen everywhere, does it? The service, I'd say, is pretty good. It's low-key, friendly and fairly efficient. Human nature being what it is, you can always offend someone, no matter how hard you try not to.

Mike Hicks, fifty-nine, was born on St Mary's to an old Scillonian farming family. He served an apprenticeship as a shipwright carpenter, was a founder member of the St Mary's Boatmen's Association in 1958, and has been its chairman since 1980. He is Vice-Chairman of the Isles of Scilly Council, is married to Jocelyn, a Scillonian, and they have five grown-up children.

Sometimes on Tresco and St Martin's, you land in one area and have pick-up points at a different place, and we have great difficulty in telling people this, because they will talk while you're trying to tell them the return times and where the pick-ups are. They sometimes swear blind they were never told, but I can categorically assure you that every boatman gives out the relevant information about return trips. Occasionally, visitors will ring me up at home when they've missed the boat back and we get saddled with going to pick them up. Most will accept it was their fault, but we have to charge them a special trip, which at the present time is £14.00. It ties up a man and a boat for at least an hour, and I think it's a fair charge. It's unfair on people if it was a genuine mistake, but sometimes, they'll get aerated and say they were never told, and you say, 'Well, you were, but didn't listen' and that can generate into an argument.

I have two sons on the boats now: Fraser, he runs the *Black Swan*, which is part of my family set-up, and Alec, who runs the *Southern Queen* on his own. I have the *Lily of Laguna*. Fraser and myself, we operate a business all the year round, and employ a couple of men as well. People think we have absolutely idyllic conditions here, and that we work a few weeks in the summer when the tourists are around, make lots of money and go to the south of France in the winter. But island life is not like that. The sea can be really bad. There's 28 miles between the two nearest points of land, the extremity of St Martin's and the extremity of Cape Cornwall, but physically we're 30 miles out in the Atlantic and when it blows hard and we have a big ground sea running, it can be very rough even between the islands.

We get councillors to and from meetings, take the first-class mail in winter from St Martin's and St Agnes, run school boats for the weekly boarders from St Martin's, shopping boats from St Martin's and St Agnes, so it's a fairly busy winter schedule. We're on a twenty-four hour call with the fire service. We're on a constant hop.

You have to be very qualified in boat handling to belong to the Association. It's easy for people to say, 'Well, that looks a good business, I'll buy a boat and join them' but if that happened, we'd have more boats than passengers. So we're very protective of what we've got. I wouldn't teach any non-islander the ropes that I taught my sons. You have to know the currents and the tide sets, the visibility can suddenly disappear and you can wind up miles from anywhere in thick fog and still have to be able to find your way back with a load of people on board without getting them excited. But there is an element of change here now.

A couple of young chaps who weren't born here are running passenger boats. They've come here to live, crewed on other boats and picked up enough knowledge to run their own. But I've never employed mainland labour myself.

The bird-watchers have certainly extended the boating season. When I first started in 1956 it was over when the schools went back early September. But the twitchers like bad weather. Last year it was mild and reasonably good so there wasn't a great deal of interest and they wandered around, a bit fed up. But when you get these gales, all sorts of things fly in, and there's a very good bush telegraph. Two or three birders will go off to each island, and if anything is spotted they get on their DC radios and hordes of them will be running down the quay, and you have a string of boats going off to look at this one bird. About three years ago there was a North American bird that appeared on Tresco, and before 9 o'clock in the morning, we had over eight hundred people there. The boats were back and forth like yo-yos.

It's a busy life here and sometimes you're under pressure, but I don't get desperately fed-up. I never want to chuck it all in and say 'to hell with it, I'm going to the mainland'. I enjoy everything I do and Scilly to me is home and a beautiful place to live. We're reasonably proud of our ancestors and I think there's about two dozen Hicks on St Mary's today. We originated from St Agnes and can trace our ancestors to 1703 when there was a fire and all the records were lost. But I would imagine we go back further than that.

John Hicks, thirty-eight, left Scilly when he was sixteen to become an apprentice engineer in Penzance for four years. He returned in 1975 to work on his father's seventy-two passenger boat. His father, whose family had been on the islands for 370 years, died in 1980 and John ran his boat for twelve years with the St Mary's Boatmen's Association. In 1993 he left the Association to work independently. He is a former councillor, runs a guest-house and gives weekly slide shows in the summer.

THE INDEPENDENT BOATMAN

My boat, *Swordfish II*, is 45 ft long and has comfortable seats under cover for twelve people, a stove, a bar, a toilet. The idea of the trip is we set off about 10 a.m., steam around looking at this and that, stop in a secluded bay for a cup of coffee and biscuits. Then we tootle on to somewhere else, passengers land on an uninhabited island where they have a run round for an hour, and I prepare the lunch. In the afternoon we land on another island for half an hour while I get the cream tea ready and we arrive back about 4.30 p.m. I probably won't make as much money doing this as I did with the Association, but that's not what I'm doing it for. There's no stress factor, it's totally relaxing and totally flexible. As long as the tides are right, we can go anywhere.

I pull the boat up at the end of October and scoot off to the mainland, hire a car and just drive around for a ten day holiday. I think everyone should get off the islands once a year to be refreshed in their mind, and know what it is they have back here. I used to go for two weeks. The first one I was quite happy, the second one I spent the entire time wishing to God I was back in Scilly. Now I do it for ten days and by the end of the first week I know I only have two or three days to go. People who don't go away very often, almost take things for granted and Scilly isn't a place where that should ever be done. It's got so many moods and different colours and nothing gives me greater pleasure than being able to share what I've got all the year round with people just here for a few days. I still get the same feeling of excitement when I round the rocks in the morning, as I do when I round the same ones in the afternoon.

It's hard work in the winter. You paint the boats, clean them up, do the Christmas lights round the town. That's something I got going about six years ago. I always used to listen to Radio Cornwall when I was doing the engines and in December there'd be Mousehole's Christmas Lights Night. I used to think, wouldn't it be nice to have lights and a carol service here. Then one year I thought, nobody else is going to do it, I'll have to. So I got hold of the chairman of the lights committee in Mousehole and said, 'What's the best way to organize Christmas lights?' And he said, 'Get a committee with at least one woman because she'll keep a bit of order and stop you all getting upset and shouting and screaming.'

So that's what I did. Now we have them all through Hugh Town, a star on the tower, a cross on the churches, and a 'Happy Xmas' 40 ft long. It's quite a sight. And what's nice is that locals who always used to go away for Christmas because it was dead flat here with just a few lights round the park are staying because they don't have to take children away to see them, and some visitors are coming for Christmas as well. I also organize a little carol service in the park; the vicar starts it, the Methodist minister finishes it, we have a few mince pies and on a good night, you might get three to four hundred people there.

THE NATURALIST

We get a tremendous mix of people on the wildlife safaris. Some are red-hot botanists and bird-watchers, others say they don't know anything about birds or flowers. So I cover everything and anything to try and give an idea of what is here, what is common, what is rare. In the plant world we've got a couple of things that don't occur on the mainland: the Dwarf Pansy and Orange Birdsfoot. In the bird world Scilly has made its name hundreds of times over. We have the first-ever record of a Chimney Swift and a Cliff Swallow from the States, the first record of a Tree Swallow, all major rarities, and we've turned them up before anyone else. We've had some from the east, too, like the Two-Barred Greenish Warbler. That arrived about six years ago and if you look it up in a book, it won't be there, it's that obscure.

During the year we have a trickle of bird-watchers, but come October, we get so many that David Hunt (whom I first worked with here) started putting big blackboards up outside the Porthcressa Restaurant with bird sightings, and held evening log calls in the disco cellar. Now I take the log call every evening. We have bird artists selling their work, a bookseller selling bird books, and another chap sells tapes of bird calls. It's a real hive of industry. Bird-watchers have a reputation for just being interested in rarities, but I get

Will Wagstaff, thirty-three, first came to Scilly for a holiday in 1975 and in 1981 ran the disco bar at the Porthcressa Restaurant, and helped with bird-watching tours. In 1989 he became Field Officer for the newly formed Isles of Scilly Environmental Trust. He is Assistant Heritage Coast Officer, the islands' bird recorder, takes visitors on wildlife safaris and gives weekly slide shows in the summer months. He is married to Maggie, with two sons.

them to count everything – Moorheads on The Pool, Sandlings on the beach, even the big flocks of Shags we had last year. I also keep a tally on the bats, butterflies, whales, dolphins and porpoises.

We had a bird here six years ago called the Caspian Plover – there'd only ever been one in Britain and that was ninety-eight years ago. About three hundred people came on the *Scillonian* (the ferry) to see it, but it only stayed a day and had gone by the time they arrived. Every now and then I just stick it in to the end of the slide show and listen to the groans and boos and hisses.

I've just started doing census work on seabirds – some of the numbers are dropping quite dramatically and the only bird that has gone up is the Fulmer. At present, Terns and Kittiwakes are giving us some concern and even Herring Gulls are dropping away. We're trying to count the Storm Petrel and Manx Shearwaters – we're catching a couple of hundred a night, putting a ring on them and measuring them, then releasing them. We'd like to find out why the numbers are decreasing and do something about it.

We've been putting down rat poison on the island of Samson because we found we were losing huge numbers of Kittiwake young. There is one stretch of cliff which for a couple of years running has had about eighty nests on it, and if they're laying two eggs each, that ought to be 160 young. They'll not all survive but we ought to get a hundred up to flying stage. But in the last couple of years we've had twelve and then about thirty. You see the young starting to come out, then a week later you see little piles of feathers near a hole and know damn well it's the rats that are doing it. We've put the best part of a ton of poison on Samson and are also doing White Island and Puffin Island – it's work that's been done elsewhere in Britain and proved successful. We don't use too high a dosage so if something eats a dead rat, it's not going to be affected. We think we've now lowered the number of rats sufficiently to give the Kittiwakes and Terns a chance.

THE DUSTMAN

Some dustmen look for treasures, but I just tipped the bins and carried on. People put out carpets, chairs and fridges and working televisions. But it's no good taking anything, if you don't want it. We have bottle banks at the back of the Town Hall, but some don't use them. We're supposed to have the most bottles in our bottle bank per head of the population as anywhere in the country. But in the summer you get more visitors than islanders which adds to the number.

I always used to take my dog Scamp along and he'd sit on the seat behind me. I'd leave the door of the dustcart open and he'd stay there. He was with me every day, rain and all. When it was wet, I put a dustbin liner over him. He was thirteen and a half when he died and he's been gone nearly eight years now. I do miss him – he was a real friend.

Everybody seems to know me. I say 'Good morning' to people and they say 'Morning, Lambert'. I suppose it's because I just speak to everybody. If I hadn't seen you before, I'd say 'Good morning' or 'Afternoon' or 'Nice day'. It doesn't cost anything to speak, does it? Even visitors stop and speak to me. Yet I'm sure if you walked down through Penzance and said 'Good morning', they'd look at you and think you're queer or something.

When I retired, the ladies all came out and gave me presents: video cassettes, half a bottle of whisky from one family, money and gift vouchers. I had scores of cards with 'We shall miss you' and all that sort of thing – I've got a big envelope with about sixty of them. Even today, people say 'We miss you'. I like to hear it said, whether they mean it or not. It's always nice isn't it?

Marian Bennett, a councillor from Bryher, wrote a poem which was read out at my retirement party and this is what it said:

Monday mornings can be bleak,
A grey start to a working week.
I drag myself up off the ferry,
The cart's on the quay, and Mr Perry.

Lambert Ernest Raymond Perry, sixty-five, was born in Cornwall and came to Scilly for a week's holiday in 1947. He decided to stay and worked on a farm for twenty years before becoming a dustman in 1973. He retired on 12 March 1993.

A wave, a smile, a cheery shout,
And suddenly the sun's come out.
Spirits lift, my steps get lighter,
You make my day a whole lot brighter.
And the wonderful service you provide
Fully justifies St Mary's pride
In a refuse collection beyond compare
To which you bring undoubted flair.
But retirement comes and it gives me pleasure,
To think of you taking well-deserved leisure.
I'm sorry I can't share this evening celebration
And that this verse lacks great inspiration.
But others will make speeches and all will make merry
To wish you all the very best – a toast to Lambert Perry.

THE PUBLICAN

Bob Hayes, thirty-nine, was a gas fitter until sixteen years ago. Unable to find work in Manchester, he came to Scilly to work as a hotel kitchen porter and, later, as a chef. He moved back to the mainland to manage pubs before returning to Scilly to the Bishop and Wolfe. He is separated from his wife and has two children.

It's a really nice way of life. I've been here eight years now and never seen a fight in the pub. I've never seen a massive argument. Once you've got to know the locals, you can have a good laugh with them and a lot of wind-ups go on, but they're really friendly. The pub we had on the mainland was the same all the time, but here you can look forward to the summer with the visitors, and at the end of that you feel you can't wait for the winter when it's all the locals playing darts and pool and enjoying themselves.

Scilly has been classed as two thousand alcoholics clinging to a rock, but that's a bit unfair. Everything revolves round the pubs, but it's more the social life than people getting drunk. There's a strong Methodist element here, and there are some who don't drink at all. Under-age drinkers don't get away with it because you know them all, but under sixteens are allowed in the Scillonian Club, so it's not too bad.

You get high spirits and I'm not trying to say there isn't trouble in the island sometimes. But you hardly ever hear of it. People come in here and they know they'll get banned if they cause trouble, and there's nowhere else for them to go. Plus they've got to see that person the next day and the day after.

There are three pubs and the nice thing is everyone wanders from one to the other – when I first came, I used to be a bit upset because all of a sudden you were busy and the next minute everyone was gone. Most people start here, wander down to the Atlantic, the Mermaid, back to the Atlantic, and then back down here for the last one.

It is a male dominated place, but saying that, women who come in here never feel uncomfortable. They meet friends and there's no aggravation at all. We get loads of women coming on their own and because everyone knows everyone, you're never going to be on your own for long.

I rowed in the gig races last year, but got chucked out of that. They said I was too old and hopeless. But I'm still involved because the pub sponsors four teams and gives them sandwiches after they've rowed and buys them a drink. In October we have a big football match against the bird-watchers, the Twitchers against the Scillies. Last year they won 4–3 and there must have been four hundred of them up there watching. That was a sight to be seen.

I'd never leave Scilly now, even if I didn't run this pub. You come out of the door and there are beaches all around you, there are beautiful walks and no trouble. I could leave the back door open and no one comes in and pinches anything. I don't think I've ever been happier anywhere in my life.

THE UNDERTAKER

I didn't have much choice really, there wasn't a lot of other work, and this is what I was brought up to do. I'm the only undertaker on all five islands and if someone dies on the off-islands, I go across to see the family and make all the arrangements for cremation, burial or sea burial. Several local people, whom you wouldn't think would want to be buried at sea, have asked if there would be any problem about it, and I told them no. Obviously you have to refer it

Alf Trenear, fifty-seven, is the fifth generation of his family to be joiners and undertakers in Scilly. He is married to Isabel and they have two children.

19

to the coroner in Penzance, and there are certain places where you go depending on weather conditions and which way the wind is. You use canvas, as on board ship. If you weighted a coffin, you wouldn't be able to manage it. The number of burials at sea has only been in the teens since I've been doing it and that's for about forty years. If people want to be cremated, I supply the coffin, and they're usually flown out by Skyvan to Land's End to my friend in Penzance, Mr Raymond Burrows, who carries out the cremation and looks after the family.

There's plenty of space for burial in the churchyard here on St Mary's, but in the off-islands it's very limited. People who come on holiday year after year sometimes ask to be buried here when they die, but they're refused now because the space is needed for an islander or long-term resident. Ashes can be scattered, though, and some people want this if they have a favourite spot, round the Garrison or facing towards Samson for instance. I carry this out for them or the family come and just quietly do it.

At one time there might have been about twenty people dying in twelve months, but now the number's gone up because there are a lot more elderly people here. But whatever I'm doing, working on a roof, for instance, and something happens, I just have to leave it.

Being an undertaker can be a stressful job, specially if it's a young person who's died. The thing is not to say too much, but listen to what the family has to say. They normally want a plain-sided coffin, but sometimes they ask for a special one with panelled sides and more expensive furnishing on handles. The coffins are made the same as they've always been except that you don't pitch the joints any more. You've got modern linings that are waterproof so you don't need to. Because of Dutch elm disease, it's difficult to get elm, so I use mahogany and oak. I've made a coffin in a day before now, but that's working perhaps from 7 a.m. to 10 p.m. for an emergency job. It normally takes two days.

I call myself an undertaker not a funeral director, as they like to be known these days, because for me, it's a part-time job. I might go six months and nothing happens, and then have three deaths in one day. As a carpenter joiner, I work on other jobs too.

It's difficult to get away but my brother-in-law can stand in for me. If I'm away for a weekend or longer, I tell the hospital so the doctors know where to contact me. It's a tied job really.

THE FORMER LIFEBOAT COX

It sounds silly to say you've never been frightened but I was never worried when I was in the lifeboat. Well, you worried that you wouldn't be able to achieve what you wanted to, but not worried for yourself though sometimes I thought afterwards, cor, I was lucky to get away with that. The most risky trip I did was when a French trawler went down on the rocks. The coastguards heard part of a Mayday message and rang us saying they believed there was a trawler aground 'on or near' the Bishop Lighthouse. So we launched and on the way heard from the Bishop that earlier they'd seen some lights coming up from the south-east, which they thought was a ship. I decided it could be, but we just didn't know where to start because 'on or near' the Bishop could be anywhere. Then some of the boys on deck said they could smell diesel oil and we saw bits of floating debris on the water although there was so much sea and water flying that it was hard to see anything. And then we saw the ship among the rocks, not more than 50 or 60 ft away, and we were trying to see how to get to it, when this big sea came in and we had to go full out to counteract it. And in a matter of that one sea, it just washed away whatever was there, and there was just a lump of the bow of the boat, about 20 or 30 ft on top of the rock, and nothing else. I think they knew we were there and had seen us coming in for them, but they'd been there possibly for an hour and a half and couldn't hang on any more. The sea just smashed the vessel up and took them with it. We found out afterwards she'd hit another rock earlier and I reckon some of them had been washed overboard before we got there.

Matt Lethbridge, sixty-nine, one of four brothers, three of whom were in the lifeboat service, has been a fisherman all his life and was a lifeboat cox for almost thirty years until he retired in 1985. His grandfather sailed in the *Cutty Sark* and a member of his family helped build the original Bishop Lighthouse. He is married to Pat and they have two daughters and three grandchildren.

21

I still think about that wreck every day. You just think, I wish I'd known this earlier, or I wish I'd done that. Well, you can't say you wish you'd done that. We went full speed all the way and went directly to it, but things happened so fast, we didn't have a chance really.

Other times we've got people in we might not have. Once my brother happened to see a light flashing and rang me. We went to the quay and there was this skipper who said he was waiting for a sailor training boat to come back. I thought, 'Oh God, I bet that's what it is', and we tore back and got the lifeboat out and found ten young people hanging on to this sunken boat. Even while we were trying to take them aboard, you can't pick up all ten at once, some of them were saying, 'Take me, I can't hold on any more.' They were in their teens and lots of them would certainly have drowned if we hadn't got there. So that was luck the other way round.

My wife and I never really wanted to go away on holiday – you were always afraid something might happen. Other people could have coped, I don't mean that, but you get so interested – the lifeboat becomes the most important thing in your life. Nowadays they are all self-righting, you have no worries at all, but ours wasn't. If it turned over, you could be down and that would be it, but you had such confidence if you handled it properly, it wouldn't. That was the thrill of it for me: that you could go out in really extreme weather and do whatever you liked with the boat, providing you used a little bit of common sense. I never eased down – we went at full speed all the time unless we were coming home, or if we were towing or searching.

My wife used to worry, of course, but with the fishing it was worrying for her anyway – it hasn't even got to be bad weather for you to get in an awful lot of trouble. You can be dragged over with the gear and so on. I nearly have, lots of times, I must admit. The wives were worse off than we were, because we knew we were alright, but couldn't tell them. When they're sitting at home and the wind's howling, it's not very nice.

THE LIFEBOAT MECHANIC AND SECOND COX

I used to go out on the lifeboat when my dad was on the crew and remember a fifteen hour trip to Brixham when I was about twelve and the boat was going for a refit. That's how you get involved, you get asked to help on the slip, and then you're roped in.

Why do I do it? I don't know. It's part of Scilly and it's nice to help the community. It's like the boys being firemen or with the ambulance. But lifeboats are a bit different, a little bit special. Courage doesn't come into it for us. I remember talking to my dad once and he said that when it was a bit hairy, he thought about it a day later.

The lifeboat, the *Robert Edgar*, is the best they could design at the time, but it's twenty years old now. We have fourteen crew on a call basis, and there's a boarding boat for getting to it. It's difficult to join the lifeboat service. You can't just come along and say, 'I want to be in it', though you can on the mainland. People are asked to join, it's put through the crew and if anyone has any objection, then that's the end of it. And the same with the cox. It's who the crew want and it's very much team work, everyone watching everyone else in case they don't see something coming.

I'm a self-taught mechanic. I've always been dealing with engines, hands on is the best way to learn anything. If we've been out, there's the brass, which has salt all over it and is tarnished, to clean – that's a good two hours' work – then there's tidying up and putting things away properly. You go through the engine and make sure the oil and water levels are alright, and the cooling system. Anything to make sure it's ready to use next time, first time. When I started, I must admit it worried me. When I got home, I used to think, what haven't I done? Maybe we're going to use it tonight and it won't work. Luckily you grow out of that and I don't worry so much now. But it drives you mad to start with.

It's a married man's job, but it's not a job that a wife enjoys. You need the support when you come back,

James Terry, thirty-one, comes from a Scillonian family and his father runs the medical launch. He works three mornings a week with the *Gry Maritha*, and rows on the *Bonnet* gig. He is divorced with a young daughter.

specially if you've been out all night, but it's not very fair on the family. You've never really got a home life as such. I have a weekend off every three weeks, but you are on call all the time. I've got my own boat, but I have to arrange for someone to cover me before I go out in it.

I do try now to make sure it is just a job, because some coxswains do go over the top and get completely absorbed with it, and that's when your other life starts to pay the price. It can become an obsession and it's knowing when to say I'm going to have a life of my own. You get the impression from the old people that the boat wouldn't go anywhere unless they were there. But as I've told my assistant, if I'm not there, I still expect the boat to go. The priority is the people the other end, but that's the modern attitude. I grew up with the old crew and the old attitude – and didn't realize it until too late.

The last wreck in Scilly was in 1972 and most of our work now is with yachts, somebody injured, gear failure, or they've lost a mast or rudder. Sometimes it's the stress of the weather and the crew can't cope any more. They can have had a good ten or twelve hours sailing from France, and if it's hard weather as well, it takes it out of you. And that's when accidents start to happen. But I wouldn't stop anyone going sailing or boating – that's where you find your limits. Everyone's sometime got to know how far you can push yourself. We never mind going out. In fact, you can ask all the boys, we enjoy what we do and the more the boat is used the better.

James Terry has since left the lifeboat service and is setting up his own business.

YOUNG SCILLONIAN

Living here is alright when you're under eleven, you can go down to the beach and the rocks, but once you're over that age, and you want to go out, there's no youth club or anything like that. I found it difficult to get through the period between eleven and fifteen, although there are water sports in the summer. But in the winter, it's just so dull, especially when you've got a gale and it's pouring with rain – there's no milk bar or anything like that. If it's not raining, I might go out with friends, and if it's a rough sea, I used to love going to the rocks and watching it. But, in another way, having nothing to do is quite useful because you might as well stay in and do school work. On the mainland, it's more difficult because there are places to go to.

I was senior manager in my last year at secondary school and through the Pupil Management Scheme we got a lot of things done that I'd wanted to see done for ages. We never had lockers before, all we had was a peg to put your coat, and a little space. We've always wanted a change in the school uniform – the girls weren't allowed to wear trousers or culottes. Now they can, and we've also got a change in the new PE kit. We organized a few charity things, and pupils versus teachers sports matches, and that was good fun. Who wins? The pupils mainly!

Robert Hale, fifteen, comes from a family which, on his father's side, goes back to 1600 on Tresco. His father runs Tremelethan Farm, and he has a younger sister of thirteen.

The Pupil Management Scheme is mainly to get pupils' ideas put through to the teachers in the right fashion, rather than have an argument with them. If we want to say something to the headmaster, we write a letter to him rather than just going and telling him. It's more formal, but the teachers seem to like it more.

I'm going to do agriculture of some kind and eventually take over the farm. I've decided that for ages now. Ever since I was about four or five I've always wanted to come back eventually, but I might get a job connected with the sale of flowers on the mainland first and try and get a broader view of the flower industry.

Why do I like it here so much? It's so relaxed, there's so little crime, you don't have to worry about being mugged or murdered. But I want to experience the mainland for a few years and the big wide world. I think Dad likes the feeling that I will take over from him, as he took over from his father. It's about 50 acres, so very small compared to the mainland, but one of the biggest over here.

Now I'm this age, it's much easier to be able to go out

with your mates; we go to the Scillonian Club. You can get junior membership and go up and play pool and darts. I enjoy playing golf, and am involved in the gigs, which takes a lot of time. We came last on Friday – it's a completely novice crew, but we're not that far behind other boats, so we're quite pleased with how we're doing. I'm the youngest at the moment. A lot of people think it's easy and just muscle, but it's not – there's so much technique to learn. In the World Championship weekend we came last out of thirty-three gigs, but we all really enjoyed it.

I've worked for Dad on the farm since I was about ten or eleven, picking flowers and just helping. I got paid a little thank-you sort of thing. Now I'm working on the farm full-time this summer which I'm really enjoying, preparing the bulbs to be planted back in the ground, or sent away to Lincolnshire. Then it's back to the old routine of cutting hedges and preparing for the flowers in mid- to late September.

I'm going to college on the mainland this autumn and I'd be a bit worried if I was going to be on my own, but I'll be with a couple of friends, so I'll be alright. I think my parents will worry, specially Mum. She says just be careful, watch your back all the time, and don't get involved in drugs or anything like that because people from here can get led on so easily. She's worried about someone bullying me because we have no experience of that here. I think there are a few bits and pieces of drugs going around here, cannabis and stuff like that, but certainly not the hard stuff like cocaine or heroin. Quite a few people drink a lot, but that's just island life really. I don't think I'll be a heavy drinker, I don't like it that much. I've had my experience of getting rather drunk and it's put me off. I'm never drinking a large amount again!

THE CHAIRMAN OF THE GIGS

The gigs are traditional boats, once the work-horses of the islands in the days before engines. They were used for carrying inter-island freight and pilot gigs for boarding ships coming in from the Atlantic. They raced in those days because they wanted to get to the ship first and put the pilot aboard – the whole crew would get a share of the money he made. That's how the racing idea started – it was to earn a living, not for pleasure.

When engines came along the gigs got laid up, but in the 1950s Newquay Rowing Club came over, found four of our old boats, bought the *Bonnet*, the *Golden Eagle* and the *Czar*, and took them back to Newquay. A few years later, the Scillonians decided they wanted to get gig racing going again, bought the boats back and built Newquay a brand-new gig in return. Since then there has been this terrific bond between the two rowing communities, and Newquay always come every September for an end of season bash.

From April to October there are two race nights a week, Wednesday for the ladies, Friday for the men. We have eight gigs – four from St Mary's, and one from each of the off-islands. The most popular course is from Nut Rock to St Mary's, but we also have races from each of the inhabited islands, and the Old Wreck Race. The gigs vary from 30 to 32 ft long and have six rowers and a coxswain. On the whole, a crew sticks to the same gig for a season, but we have a series of swap races when they all change gig because they do vary quite a bit, from the *Bonnet*, built in the 1830s, to one built in the 1980s. But at the end of the day, it's the crew that makes the difference.

The big thing we've got every year now is the World Championships. The idea came from a chap called Grant Tucker. He was walking down the road one day looking at all the vacancy signs, and he said to his wife, 'Why don't we have a championship over here and get lots of gigs over?' It was discussed at the next committee meeting, and we decided to have a big event and call it a world championship. It was a little bit tongue in cheek to start with, organized as a one-off. We had a Dutch crew come over that year and since then we've had American crews, all keen to come back though they haven't managed it yet. People always ask, 'How do you justify calling it a world championship?' The answer is because anyone who can turn up with a six-oared gig from anywhere in the world is

Jeremy Phillips, thirty-six, was born on Scilly, joined the Merchant Navy, and in 1983 returned to work here. He is married to Karen, and they have three daughters. He can trace his ancestors back eight generations. He now runs the *Kingsley II* passenger boat and is Chairman of the Gig Racing Association.

quite welcome to take part. It's a terrific spectator sport.

The boats were built for use in open water and often had to go out in rough weather. We'll happily row in anything up to a force 6 or 7, and I've been out in gigs in fresher weather than that. You go out practising on a really rough night, row right into it, and then turn round and run right back on the big sea. The boat just takes itself, just flies down the waves. All you have to do is keep the oars going.

THE FLOWER FARMER

Andrew May, thirty-nine, was born on Scilly, studied Economics at Nottingham University, worked in marketing, and when his father retired, he returned to Scilly to take over his 60 acre flower farm. He set up Mainland Marketing Ltd, a company funded by growers to sell and organize the transport of flowers in the UK and mainland Europe, and is on the steering committee of an Education and Business Partnership. He is married to Juliet and they have three sons.

There must be fifty or so flower farmers on the islands today and there is a thriving flower industry, but it's true to say it isn't as profitable as it used to be and most of us do other things as well, out of necessity.

From all five islands, we send out sixty thousand boxes of daffodils and narcissi a year to the rest of the UK and Europe, and there are about six hundred flowers in one box. There are twenty thousand registered names of individual varieties but *Soleil d'Or* is what the industry has been built on, and is the best known. It's yellow with an orange centre that deepens on maturity, but the main thing is it has a lovely scent. It *is* a very good flower and that's why we're successful and command a bit of a premium in the market place.

Local growers here now run a research station, Trenoweth Research and Development Ltd, to improve the quality of existing varieties and to establish new ones – the company grew from the ashes of Government-backed experimental horticultural stations that were shut down. That was three years ago now, but with some help from the Government and a lot of help from the Duchy and others, we raised funds to form this new company which is much more finely tuned to our needs. It is very necessary to have it because of the pressure on us to change.

Flowers from all over the world are now being sent to the UK and although I think the amount we send is going up, the price is going down and we're finding it difficult to produce flowers cheaply enough. Of course, the bigger you are, the lower your unit costs, so small family farms are being squeezed. There's one farm in Penzance whose annual output of flowers is the same as all the islands here put together.

I make a point of having flowers available right through the spring season – we start exporting in November, even October, and finish early April because the market is very volatile and there's nothing more infuriating than having a lull when one crop is finished, the market picking up and you having nothing to send. When we've finished picking, we harvest early potatoes, and then go straight into the bulb season, which is actually the busiest time of the year. We sell about 20 tons of bulbs a year; the rest are planted back.

In the frost of 1986/7, when temperatures were very low, we lost over 3 km of sheltered hedging and over ten thousand trees on this farm alone. It's taken us the last five years to remove tons of dead wood, and we're now re-planting. We've worked very hard but it will be another five years before we get an iota of benefit from it. Ten years is a very long-term investment, but you do it because you live here, want to be growing flowers in ten years' time, and they won't be of the quality they should be if you don't.

There are four of us full-time on the farm, but in the harvest we take on two or three more people to pick flowers, and seven or eight to bunch them. Some get lily rash on the skin from the juice of the daffodils, but it's never affected me. Many people are attracted by the notion of being on an island and picking flowers, but when they come for a job, you know within five minutes whether they're going to be any good or not. It's physically quite demanding – you're bending over all the time – and it requires a certain mental state of mind. You have to be prepared to get stuck in and suffer some initial discomfort. When it's blowing half a gale and there's a great deal of pressure to get the crop into the packing shed, it's not the most enjoyable way to spend an afternoon. But on a nice sunny day, even in the middle of February, it can be absolutely glorious, warm and sunny with fabulous colours and views. And one of the great joys of it is that, after a few days when you've got the hang of what you're doing, you can lose yourself in your own world and have time to think.

THE MEDICAL LAUNCH BOATMAN

Rodney Terry, fifty-eight, was born on Tresco. He spent two years in the Royal Navy, five in the Merchant Navy, and worked on St Mary's quay for thirty years. He was lifeboat cox for six years, and second pilot for the island. He is married to Ann Jenkins, whose family on Bryher goes back four generations, and they have three grown-up children.

The medical launch is a 29 ft Chiverton, owned by the Medical Launch Trust. I'm on call twenty-four hours a day, seven days a week and have a pager in my pocket so I can move around a bit. But if I want to go off the island, or go out in my own boat, I have to get someone to stand in for me which can be a bit of a problem sometimes. The doctors have regular services to the off-islands three times a week and the district nurse usually goes once a week. I take them across and wait for them to come back. We have a helicopter cover on the mainland, but usually go ourselves.

We came close to a baby being born on the boat one day – it was left a little bit late when I was called. I went off as quick as possible to Tresco and was almost there when I got this call to say where was I, the lady had gone into labour? I picked her up and dashed back and an hour and a half later the baby was born. That was near enough. But you have to be a bit careful. The launch is not a lifeboat, just an ordinary boat. We've got radar, which is a great help, and if you've been round the islands all your life, the instinct is there anyway. But in a lifeboat you have six or seven other chaps with you, in the medical launch you're on your own. In an emergency the doctor comes with me and if anyone is wheelchair bound, people will give a hand and get them aboard. With broken bones, they call out the coastguard and get the patient on a stretcher. The worst thing that happened was when a man died on the boat. He had been ill for a long time and I think he didn't actually want to come to hospital. In the event, I had to go and get him with the doctor, and his wife and son and daughter were on the boat as well. He was keen on the gigs, he coxed the Tresco gig for many years, and he actually passed away right on the line where the gigs start at Nut Rock. I think it was what he would have wanted.

THE LAUNDRETTE LADY AND ENTERTAINER

When I first came here, I thought it was Sicily. I'd been on holiday to Spain with my family and thought it would be marvellous to work abroad. I answered an ad for a girl to help in a hotel and it was dreadful at first, but after a couple of weeks, I thought it was lovely. You can be more natural here and the people are very genuine. It's like a big family, everyone is so supportive. If you don't try and put on airs and graces, I think they take to you. My sister says I could never live back on the mainland again and I couldn't.

When I got divorced I thought I'd better get a full-time job and that's when I started at the laundrette and petrol station. I've been there eighteen years now. I do the petrol, take gas and coal orders. The laundrette side is a service laundry in so far as people are not allowed to do it themselves, we do it for them. Visitors bring their washing in the morning and fetch it when they come off the boats in the afternoon. It used to be terribly busy, but now a lot of holiday lets are providing their own washing machines and hotels and guest-houses are putting in their own laundries. I suppose it's a bit cheaper. It's quiet in the winter, but you see islanders on a regular basis and the same people come back every year on holiday.

The Theatre Club put on a play in the summer and a pantomime in the winter. The Entertainers is like a concert party, they do shows throughout the summer with a different theme each year. I sing, but it's not beautiful singing, it's like music hall. I usually do funny songs because I have a very loud voice. It's great fun and the visitors love it. They come as children, and now they're grown up and married and they still come. It's part of Scilly really. We get full houses, and all the money goes to local charities. If anyone needs anything or has a problem they come to The Entertainers. Next year will be our fortieth anniversary.

Some wives whose husbands have come here to work are not so happy. Perhaps there aren't enough shops, you are

Maggie Perkovic, fifty-three, lived in Hemel Hempstead before coming to Scilly in 1960 to work in a hotel. She is divorced and has four grown-up children.

thrown back on your own resources. You get a gale ripping through in the winter and you can't get very presentable because you're blown to pieces. On a foggy day in the winter, there's no flying, no letters, no papers, you are a bit cut off. But it depends how you feel. I think it's quite nice – it's just us again. Or perhaps it's because I've been here thirty-two years now and am getting used to it.

THE BOAT BUILDER

Tom Chudleigh, seventy, is a Scillonian five or six generations back. His great-great-grandfather was married to the daughter of the steward of Star Castle when it was a garrison, his grandfather was a stonemason and helped build the church on Tresco and the Town Hall on St Mary's. He started work in the Shipwright Department of the Steamship Company, but forty years ago left to set up on his own and has been building boats, figureheads, 'anything with timber' ever since. His wife, Ethel, helps with the boatbuilding.

I've built a few houses and bungalows when the boat work was slack but I'd rather do the boats, it's more interesting, they're all different. I've made sailing boats, motor boats and gigs – the longest rowing boat we do is 32 ft. The last gig I did took twelve months exactly, but I did a few other little jobs in between, mind. I work with my better half, she helps with the riveting and painting. There are four thousand rivets in a gig and someone has to hold the dolly on the outside, so Ethel's the 'go for', 'get me this' girl.

Originally, the boats were all built from Cornish elm – it's tough and will stand quite a bit. The grain is all over the place, so if the gig rests on a sharp stone on the beach, it won't split very far. Dutch elm disease ruined all the trees though I've built three gigs with whych elm from Shropshire and it seems to be wearing just the same. A lot depends on how the boats are cared for. Years ago, they were kept in thatched boat-houses which I think were better than the tile roof ones they use today. The thatch was warmer in winter and cooler in summer. But I don't think the Duchy would like that now.

I've built seven gigs – I'm the only one doing it on Scilly, the others have got more sense – and never was anything written down, no contracts. But the money has always come through. When I built the first one in 1967 for £501 – it was the first to be built here for nearly a hundred years – the coxswain used to come along and say, 'I suppose you could do with a bit of cash?' And I'd say, 'Yes.' And he'd go to the bank and transfer some money from the gig account to ours, and that was it until the gig was finished and then the balance was paid over. I never worried it wouldn't come. Some people say there's no hurry west of the Tamar and there may be something in it. If they're going to do something, they'll do it directly, which can be any time.

I built the first here in this glasshouse which belonged to a farmer. He loaned it free of charge and I've been renting it from the Council for the last fourteen years or longer. Now we're making a boat for ourselves, the *Mary M*, but I won't live long enough to build all the boats I'd like to, though I couldn't make anything very big because I don't have the premises. I've beaten my head against a wall for over thirty years to buy my own, but have got nowhere with the Council or the Duchy, they just won't have it. I don't know why, I'm sure. Retire? I get tired, perhaps, but I don't know about retired. What would I do if I gave up boatbuilding? It's always been boats with me.

THE DUCHY OF CORNWALL LAND STEWARD

The Duchy office is in what was once part of the military garrison and Augustus Smith lived here before building the Abbey on Tresco in the mid-nineteenth century. It's been a hotel, and was used in the war by the military. There is a holiday flat for Duchy staff and others, and two residential flats. Prince Charles comes quite frequently but Tamarisk, locally known as his holiday cottage, is let as required to Royal Household, or senior Duchy staff.

The Duchy owns all the Isles of Scilly except for Hugh Town and a few freehold properties on St Mary's, and runs the pier and harbour. We lease Tresco to Robert Dorrien Smith, and much of the untenanted land and uninhabited islands to the Environmental Trust.

The total District revenue for 1992 was about £440,000 and we have turned around a deficit that had run for many years to a small profit, by a mixture of good housekeeping, and by the

Lt.-Col. Ian Robertson, sixty-one, served in the Argyll and Southern Highlanders from 1950 to 1979. He and his wife lived in six countries before he became the Duchy of Cornwall Land Steward here in 1980.

33

fact that residential rents of properties have risen very dramatically over the last ten or twelve years. The chief sources of income are rentals from fifty flower farms, residential and commercial properties, the pier and harbour and other items.

We've sold about £1 million of property to cover more than our total capital expenditure for improvements on properties and farms, we've balanced the books on the capital side, and changed the revenue side around so we're no longer a drain on the resources of the Duchy. In many cases it has been uncomfortable, but I think most people understand it is inevitable. In the past, rents here were very low, but so was the input by the Duchy and I think there's an understanding now that rents have got to be reasonable. We endeavour to provide a service to all our tenants so if something needs doing or goes wrong, we can put it right fairly promptly, and we have improved the standard of many of the houses in recent years.

Basically, Scilly is a non-development area and, as a result, freehold and leasehold house prices are very high, as high as in London, which makes it extremely difficult for local people to buy one. It is now Duchy policy to ensure that all property let or sold is on the basis of full-time residential occupation, although this was not always the case before 1980. Some 30 per cent of properties on the islands are still second homes and this, I think, is awful.

We spend a lot of time and money clearing old trees and planting new strips. I would like to do more, but it's always a question of balance. I could do with a few extra hundred thousand pounds and a quicker growing season. We mostly plant the Monterey pine which grows fairly straight and stands the salt spray and wind. The amount of salt in the atmosphere virtually kills everything else.

The Scillonians, as all islanders, like to grumble a bit – quite rightly – and the ones they like to have a go at, in no particular order, are the Council, the Steamship Company, the Duchy, and now the Environmental Trust. But I manage to live with it, and sleep well at night. In a conservation area, everyone is fighting to do what they want to do. People who ride their horses sometimes go across footpaths, which makes a mess; other people want to ride their motorbikes, which makes a noise; others want to go shooting, which disturbs people who go walking or riding. A lot of activities are fine for those who enjoy them, but not always for everyone else. You have to have a considerable degree of live and let live over here.

I suppose the main difference between this job and the Army, where one tended to give orders and expect them to be obeyed, is that here you spend more time talking and discussing things, and hope to come up with something that will be accepted. You never know, you might want to be rescued when both boat engines stop the next day!

If I had to name one achievement I've had in Scilly, it was bringing cricket back to the off-islands. When I arrived none of them played and hadn't done for many years. I took teams to St Agnes and St Martin's in the early years and it's now flourishing.

Colonel Robertson retired in October 1993.

THE MAN WITH A VARIED LIFE-STYLE

We left Bryher for an easier way of life. We were market gardening there for twenty-five years and that included fishing and anything that happened to be going. It was hard work and long hours, but we liked the life-style, that was the attraction. Our life was our work.

We'd start sending narcissi to the mainland around the second week of December, and different varieties followed one behind the other, until Easter. Then there was early potatoes which took up about two or three weeks and irises. During the winter, we'd do netting at night for grey mullet. We'd start lobster potting about the first of April and that would carry on until the end of September. Bulbs would be lifted and replanted from about 1 June, and hopefully finished by the end of August. Then it would be a clean up job through

Brian Jenkins, fifty-eight, lived and worked on Bryher until sixteen years ago when he and his wife, Clare, moved to St Mary's. He's fished and farmed, was the medical launch boatman, an auxiliary fireman and coastguard, undertaker's assistant, and a Customs' representative. He is married, has two grown-up children and now runs a guest-house with his wife.

the autumn, fence trimming, you know what I mean, the green fences (hedges), and we pulled a lot of seaweed from the beach. I worked single-handed for about fifteen years after my father retired and I'd put about 150 tons of seaweed a year on the empty land we'd lifted from bulbs.

That's what I mean by an interesting life-style. And there would be all sorts of other jobs that would come into it. We always had our own boat and in the '50s and '60s, we'd fetch a lot of our own provisions like oil and coal from St Mary's.

We had this house built in 1964 so we knew we hoped to come, but didn't know when. Now we run a guest-house and in my spare time I go fishing. Stocks are very low, and will be so for the rest of my life and a long time after. Too many are chasing too few. It's as simple as that. Fishing isn't a thing you recommend to anyone. If they want to do it, they'll do it. In the likes of my case, I've known people come here year after year and they say, 'You're still going then?' and I say, 'Yes, I'm still going.' And I quite often say, 'If you've been on drugs for fifty years, you'd have a job to give it up', and that's the best way I can explain it. You get threadbare with it. You come home tired and teasy and think you'd like to give it up but by the time you've had your dinner and an hour's rest, you're ready to have another look to see what it's going to be like tomorrow.

I like doing the guest-house very much. At the beginning, I thought if I don't get it right, too bad, I'll learn as I go along. Now, if you put the sausages I've cooked down end to end, there'd be enough to go round the world. Clare does the serving and if there's beds to change, I help her. I'd get a degree in hoovering!

There's hardly a day goes by when I don't do something. Last winter a younger man with a bigger fishing boat than mine rang me up and said he was hoping to go on fishing till Christmas if he could find someone to go with him. I said, 'I know I'm an old cripple, but would I do?' 'I should think you'd do very well,' he said. And I went with him until New Year. Then, I was on the beach one day and the same man came up to me and said, would I like an indoor job for a bit? And I said, 'What's on?' 'Well,' he said, 'demolition for starters.' I said, 'I'm good at that.' And yes, I'd come. And I worked with him on a building site for three months.

If in seven or eight years' time I don't feel like taking part in the fishing, I shall want to be watching it and seeing it. A lot of my cronies, all outdoor men of course, thought I was mad when I left Bryher, but I'm not sure they would think so now.

THE STEAMSHIP COMPANY
MANAGING DIRECTOR

The Isles of Scilly Steamship Company was founded over seventy years ago to establish a regular freight service to Penzance. In those days, the islanders exported a lot of flowers and potatoes, and needed a regular lifeline, so a group of them got together to set up the company and it's been carried on by Scillonians ever since.

The current passenger vessel is *Scillonian III*, fourteen years old and able to carry six hundred passengers, but for the last five years, it hasn't operated in winter. The *Gry Maritha*, bought from Norway four years ago, now does three trips a week throughout the year and carries about 10,000 tons of cargo. It can also take about twelve passengers. Before we had the *Gry Maritha*, everything came on the *Scillonian*. She was built to carry containerized cargo and did it reasonably successfully, but with changes in operating costs and the way in which cargo was presented, it became necessary to improve our freight service. Now the *Scillonian* carries about 3 tons of freight a day, 600 to 700 tons a year, most of it perishable stuff, and the odd car and passenger boats. Last year, there were about sixty thousand passengers from Easter to October.

A few years ago the company set up the Isles of Scilly Skybus to operate a fixed-wing aircraft. In 1992 it carried about thirty thousand passengers, second-class mail and parcels. There's no transport to the islands on a Sunday and the airport is closed to give islanders peace from the noise of aircraft. But more people do expect to travel on

Kenneth Christopher, fifty-five, is a Scillonian whose family have lived in Scilly for several generations. He trained as an agriculturalist at Seale Hayne Agricultural College, worked for the Ministry of Agriculture as a farm advisor, and for twenty years was estate manager on Tresco before moving to St Mary's. He is married to Corinna, who works as the Steamship Company's office manager, and they have two daughters. He spends two days a week in the company's Penzance office, is a councillor and plays the church organ when the organist is on holiday.

this day and maybe it's something they will have to look at again.

An ordinary return on the *Scillonian* is £60; on Skybus it's £72 and we do quite a lot of family discounts. If Mum and Dad and two children book on the *Scillonian*, they can get a 20 per cent reduction. But nowadays a lot of people prefer to fly and, of course, it gives you a longer time here if you're only coming for the day, though in my opinion, coming by sea is the real way to approach the islands. The amount of day trippers has fallen in the last two years because there haven't been the number staying in Cornwall. It is expensive to get here, but you have to remember that the islands are small and the *Scillonian* costs probably £10,000 a day to run, whether you're carrying two people or six hundred. If we reduced the fares? The day trip is the same as it has been for three years. We offer certain reductions at certain times, but our experience is that if you halved the fare, you wouldn't get twice the number of people. We've tried. The other problem is that if the 'stoppers' (people who come and stay as opposed to day trippers) and day trippers were all travelling on the same boat, and you halved the day trip fare, there would be enormous disparity between the two.

At present, we're trying to acquire a Twin-Otter aircraft which is a nineteen-seater. That's about the largest you can get into St Mary's because of the size of the runway. Luggage is always a problem and weight loading is quite critical with small aircraft. We trim the plane up by distributing the weight of passengers to improve its operational characteristics.

There are no plans for the *Scillonian* to finish. All ships have a viable and economic life and it will eventually have to be replaced, as our other ships have had to be. But because we've been laying her up in the winter, we've actually extended her life by several years. She's certainly got another ten years of operation, and of course, she's completely free of any mortgage or debt. Provided we can keep a reasonable number of passengers, and keep it viable, there seems to be no reason why we shouldn't carry on. If and when we do replace her, we would try and go for something that has better sea-keeping qualities. If you can do the journey more quickly and comfortably, we might attract more people back.

THE CAPTAIN

The present *Scillonian* can take six hundred passengers and about 180 tons of cargo, with an average crew of nineteen in the height of the summer. We have a bar and buffet and, since last year, provide cooked meals. It's a totally different ship from its predecessor – far bigger, more modern though it's sixteen years old now, and stabilized which the other one wasn't. But trade has dropped off and a few years ago, Management decided it would be more economic to lay it up in the winter, and buy a cargo ship, the *Gry Maritha*, to bring cargo in all the year round. If it breaks down, or for whatever reason doesn't come, we have continued the service for short periods. We do our maintenance on the *Scillonian* in winter – it's very much an office job for me then. We paint the ship right through and I help wherever I can but I must admit I much prefer it when we sailed all the year round. Working on the sea was my job, that's why I went to sea.

Captain Paul Row, fifty, was born in Ludgvan near Penzance, went to a sea training school near Southampton, joined the Blue Star Line for ten years and in 1970 began work with the Isles of Scilly Steamship Company on *The Queen of the Isles*. He was Mate on *Scillonian II* and *Scillonian III*, and in 1977 took over as Master. He is married and has two children.

Our waters are very exposed to the Atlantic seas and if there's a westerly gale, we have a very big sea. Occasionally, we have problems with ships that either under-estimate our speed or don't realize we may be carrying on to the west. As we come away from Land's End, we cross over a north–south traffic separation scheme, and in general ships approach it, turn north and go up through the lanes, whereas obviously we have to carry on across to the west. Many don't appreciate this, and hang on, so we blow our whistle and take avoiding action.

One good thing about being Master of this ship is that I've got a home life as well as being a sailor. In my ten years deep sea, I was only home for a few weeks a year, now I'm home (on the mainland) almost every day though I sleep aboard three or four nights a week.

THE ENVIRONMENTALIST

Humfrey Wakefield, sixty-eight, was brought to Scilly on holiday when he was one and continued to come almost every year until in 1956 he came to live in the family house leased from the Duchy. He is a potter, a founder member of the Isles of Scilly Environmental Trust and its Deputy Chairman. He is married to Helena, an artist.

I decided Scilly was too good a place to miss so at the end of the war I thought up a scheme for making a living here. I was an archaeologist specializing in fifth-century BC Greek pottery until I got interested in how it was made, went on a fortnight's course to find out what you needed to be a potter and started from scratch. My wife had artistic leanings, so she did the art work, and we've been making a living out of it ever since. I make mead too. Spread it around a little, do a bit of barter.

Nine years ago the Council decided to set up an Environmental Trust and asked various people if they would like to be founder members of it. I thought I'd never done anything in public life here – I'm a naturalist, the old-fashioned kind, and I thought naïvely that the Trust would be a body to look after that sort of thing. But almost the year it was formed, it got deeply involved in politics. The issue was about putting rubbish on Barr Point, a notable beauty spot and there was a great outcry about it. Of course, the Trust were against it. We felt out of our depth and became very unpopular. But we won because the project proved to be unworkable. Then there was the building of St Martin's Hotel. The Duchy were behind that, because their business is to make money out of the islands regardless, as far as I can see, of conservation. But the hotel ran out of stone for facing the building, and wanted to take some from the old 'hedges', as Scillonians call the walls around the fields. They are almost totally overgrown with bracken, so you can't see them, and they only wanted to take the top layer. But because one of the objectives of the Trust is about preservation of archaeological remains, we had to say no. I'm not sure I wasn't for taking the stone because the hotel was three-quarters built, and it would be better if it looked right, even if it was at the expense of those walls, as against importing stone, which wouldn't have done. But I think I was in a minority. The Duchy over-rode us, and there was a great outcry and everyone said what was the good of the Trust if we had no teeth, and were just pawns of the Duchy?

But we've had easier subjects, like what you do if hedgehogs go ramping round as they are, and the fact that rats have absolutely ruined Samson for bird life, and that Greater Black-backed Gulls have been long-standing destroyers of bird life here. These are easily dealt with because they're quite specific. Well, not easily, because if anyone hears that a ton of Warfarin has been put down on Samson, they'll say this is ethnic cleansing. And when they hear the black-backs on Annet have been poisoned, they'll say how disgusting, it's a beautiful bird. It was a very rare bird sixty years ago, people came here to see it, but it settled in and multiplied exceedingly and caused colossal damage. Then there's the Yorkshire Fog on Annet, a type of grass that is burying everything under it. Dogs are a terrible problem and we started a dog control campaign, giving out poop scoops. The biggest complaint from the Tourist Association questionnaires was about dogs. The next was traffic – vehicles are badly maintained so they stink, and the big trucks with hydraulic hoists are out of scale.

I think it's the Trust's job to keep an eye on these things and then either do something about them, or tell the body concerned that they have to. We're a thorn in their sides, and I think we should be. I'm not interested in the administrative side and if I see figures, I go into a terminal decline – I leave it to people who understand them. They don't know how to stick handles on mugs and I do.

I thought of the Trust as a sort of think-tank, a watch dog and a body of people who have specialized knowledge. I never thought we'd be landed in these massive arguments about matters involving huge amounts of money. If you're going to live here happily, you've got to get on with everyone, keep your head below the parapet. When the Duchy put all untenanted land in the hands of the Trust, they, along with other bodies, said, why aren't you doing this or that, which they hadn't done before, and trustees could be walking down the street and be nobbled and sworn at. This is a painful thing though I've got quite used to it now.

But the good thing about the Trust is that it's a much more democratic body to have looking after the land than the Duchy. They were autocratic and in a sense benign in that they did nothing. It's what we call benign neglect. Which is probably a very good thing in a place like this. It's been going on for centuries with no one cutting paths or preserving ancient monuments, because they weren't at risk until the tourist trade started. That's no disrespect to the tourist, but simply pressure of feet. The islands are so small it doesn't take a lot of people to start damaging them.

THE HEAD TEACHER

Alun Howells, fifty-three, was born in South Wales, took a BA in English and History at the University of North Wales and a Diploma of Education at the University of Wales, Cardiff. He taught for three years at a boys' grammar school in Norfolk and at twenty-six came to Scilly with his young family to be in charge of the English Department at the new comprehensive school. He became Head Teacher in 1990, after a few years as Deputy Head.

At present we have 120 children from eleven to sixteen. It's a genuine comprehensive school in the sense that the number of youngsters who choose to go to independent mainland schools is very small. The trend is for them to go from here at sixteen to further education and training on the mainland, which is quite a challenge for them because from the time they're born, apart from the one or two who come to the islands during their school career, they spend all their time here with the same group of young people. This means when you see our Year 7 group, that's all the eleven- and twelve-year-old children on the islands, all together in one class. This is pretty unusual I should think.

All the teaching staff are on pretty close terms with our parents and can talk to almost all of them on first name terms. We're all part of the community and reliant on each other. And although we're experts in our own particular educational fields, we know darn well that the parent sitting in front of us could well be, for example, the person on whom we rely when we're out on the water.

I think you'll find youngsters here are generally confident in themselves. Having small groups in school does mean they have a lot more personal attention and contact with teachers so there isn't too much of a 'them' and 'us' situation. They're not street-wise in the sense city children would be, but nowadays with television, newspapers, and late-teenagers coming to work here, they do come up against some of the problems that occur on the mainland. All we can do is give them as much sensible information and advice as possible. We take them to Devon and Cornwall for work experience, to the Sheffield area for a cultural study week, and to Dartmoor for Duke of Edinburgh award expeditions.

Yes, the Isles of Scilly School came top of the published league tables of GCSE results last year, but I'm sceptical about these tables and, as I've said on TV and radio, the whole thing must be treated with the greatest caution. The results were published on an Authority basis, so if you take Cornwall, you'd have one school with a certain percentage, another would put their figures in, and there would be an average between the two. The Isles of Scilly LEA came out top because we are the only school – we didn't have any others to boost or reduce our figure, which was just over 75 per cent of our youngsters achieving Grade C or above.

But I wouldn't want anybody on the mainland to come away with the false assumption that we are a high middle-class society in which all the parents are well off. That's far from the case. Average wages on the Scillies are low and those well-off people who have come to the islands have very little to do with the school – they'll have bought holiday cottages here or retired.

We had eighty firm applications for the last two staff posts we advertised. I certainly try to make sure they realize life here is not going to be one long holiday; that they shouldn't come if they have personal family problems and think they can sort them out here, because island life puts a spotlight on them straight away. It's important there's a family commitment, that they know the advantages and disadvantages of teaching in a small school, not the least of which is that on occasions we can be completely cut off and you can walk down the street one winter evening and meet nobody at all.

THE POETS

Lady Wilson, the wife of former Prime Minister Lord Wilson, was born in Diss, East Anglia, the daughter of a Congregational minister. She and Lord Wilson first came to Scilly in 1952, and later bought a bungalow here. Lady Wilson has had several books of poetry published, is President of the Ladies' Lifeboat Guild and has two sons and twin daughters.

Lady Wilson: We were to have come here on our honeymoon because we had heard it was pretty. And then the war started, so we couldn't come. When my husband's parents moved down to Cornwall, we came and stayed at the Star Castle for a week and decided we never wanted to go anywhere else. After a few years we got the bungalow. We named it Lowenva which I think is supposed to mean House of Happiness.

Now we come whenever we can and I'm involved in the life of the islands a little. We go to everything we can that is Scillonian. The islanders have always been very good to us, and we've always done what we could for them. When there was more publicity, they used to be very protective and tell people they should leave us alone when we were on holiday. It's funny now when we go down the street because people who come off the boat say 'Good Morning, Sir,' to my husband, and I think, 'Oh here goes, Mrs Nobody again' [laughs]. I don't mind because the islanders know me and he doesn't know them quite so well as I do. So it's a very nice division.

We live in a flat in London which is nice enough for all the things we have to do, but this is home. When we first came, it reminded me so much of East Anglia – I think it's because of the sky. There is such an enormous amount of it here, as there is there. And the air is so clear. I'm sure this makes people vivacious because I notice that those who come and live here from the mainland get this vivacity too. When you come off the helicopter you can smell the air; I've heard people say it's like wine. I hang washing out on the line and it rains on it, and then it blows on it, and then the sun shines on it, and it comes in white as snow.

I've been writing poetry since I was about six. I think people write whether they are going to get it published or not. But I don't write very much now, I don't have time. I think it's such a shame people say they can't stand Shakespeare because they had to learn great chunks of it at school. If you did have to learn it, you always have it.

When I go for walks now, I'm mentally reciting poetry to myself all the time, usually rather war-like things like, 'There's a breathless hush in the Close tonight, Ten to make and the match to win'. I could quote poetry for an hour without stopping, but I can't add two and two together, though both my sons are mathematicians.

When I'm in London I often think about all my friends here, and a lot about my ladies in the Ladies' Lifeboat Guild. If I'm in trouble, I sometimes ring up the Methodist minister. I think of the islands and the beauty of them, and going on the boats. It's lovely in winter too. I remember one Christmas Day we were eating sandwiches outside. Of course, you get gales, and if you read my poems in *A Journey to Scilly*, I describe how all the boats are drawn up, the restaurants and hotels closed, people meeting each other more than they do in summer, and everyone busy getting ready for the next season with painting and decorating. The various organizations all have their dinners and I go to the lifeboat one if I'm here. I remember once when we were going back to the mainland, and somebody said to me, 'The days will soon be drawing in, me dear. Yes, we'll soon have the islands to ourselves again.' It was a bit as if we couldn't get away quick enough to let islanders have the islands to themselves [laughs].

If you come at Easter and the daffodils are still out, you approach the church and can smell the flowers before you get there. I go up to Buzza Hill on Easter Sunday at 6.30 in the morning, with the Methodist choir, and we sing 'Christ the Lord Is Risen Today', we have a prayer and a reading. It's a wonderful little service. Then we go to the Anglican church later in the morning, and the Methodist chapel in the evening, so we certainly celebrate Easter.

Every night I go out of the bungalow and look that way to see the sea, and this way I can see the lighthouse going round. I like to come out and look at the stars. You can't see stars in London.

Tony Armstrong: I don't think I read a serious book until I was about twenty and went into the Army. One day I was

Tony Armstrong, sixty-one, came to Scilly from Yorkshire in 1960 to work as a chef. He has been a flower picker, dustman, builder, and is now a chef at the Bell Rock Hotel. He is married to artist Diana French, and has three daughters.

working in my father's bakery and I picked up the *Daily Mirror*. Cassandra, a marvellous journalist, had a series running called 'Genius of the Year' and he'd nominated Dylan Thomas. He quoted a few lines from 'Death shall have no dominion' and this so knocked me out I thought, 'Well, I'd better start reading this guy.' So I did, and other verse and decided to do English 'A' Level at night school.

When I'd read quite a lot, my road to Damascus, if you like to call it, I started writing poetry myself. I met an editor who happened to be bringing out a book called *The Wind and the Rain* and he took one of my poems. I've been publishing them in *The Scillonian* magazine since 1962 so that's become quite an institution. This year, it's the 400th anniversary of the Star Castle, and the first person they came to was me. It's like medieval times – if you wanted a bucket mended you went to the bucket mender; if you wanted a ballad you went to the local poet. This is what it's like in an island community.

In 1985 I was fortunate enough to be published in *Poetry Review* which is like the Royal Academy of verse. I was working at The Galley restaurant, frying fish and chips, the editor had sent me a load of copies so I thought I might sell them there. One day in walked an American who asked what a poetry magazine was doing in a fish shop. I said I was selling it, he asked why, and I said because I had a poem in it. He bought a copy and came back to say he would mention it to the poetry editor of Radio 3. A year later the BBC rang and said they wanted to do a half-hour programme, *Poetry for Supper*, about my life. They came down and recorded it and I got quite a bit of attention then.

I travel quite a bit now, but I always feel a bit of a charlatan if I write about a landscape I don't belong to. I wrote a lot of poems in retrospect about Yorkshire but it was a long time before I could write about Scilly. It's strange that.

THE CHIEF EXECUTIVE

It's a remarkable position because although the Council is very small, it has the power of a County and District Council. We're the last public sector water authority in England and Wales, an airport authority, and are responsible for education, agriculture, welfare, the police and planning. Although we're not like the Channel Islands or the Isle of Man with our own parliamentary system, we do have to be deliberately included in local government legislation. Some laws don't apply here, some have been adapted. The most obvious example is that there are no MOTs.

It's very interesting for me to be working directly with government – normally a chief executive works more through local authority organizations. Even more interesting is that this kind of one-tier system, which has operated for a hundred years in the Isles of Scilly, is now the preferred model for the whole of the UK. We have twenty-one councillors, thirteen from St Mary's and two each from the other islands and no party political labels, which creates a continuity of policy – it's perfectly possible for two members to be in absolute agreement about one issue, and absolute disagreement on the next, but in a civilized way. There is a focussing around issues with each one having a different grouping of members.

Education is a truly community issue. In fact Scilly had the earliest example of compulsory education in Europe. It goes back to 1834 when Augustus Smith built a school, employed qualified teachers, and had a secular curriculum. Children learnt English and maths whereas most free education at that time was from the Bible Society. Augustus Smith made it compulsory from the age of two to thirteen by charging parents $1d$ a week if children went to school, $2d$ if they didn't. That has left an almost cultural value of education here. It's seen as a foundation for individual and community prosperity, and the Authority today provides an additional resource into education that many others wouldn't. We spend £1 million a year from central government and add about £100,000 to that.

Philip Hygate, thirty-five, is Chief Executive and Chief Education Officer of the Isles of Scilly Council. He has a degree in Economics and Political Economy, has worked for the Open University, and set up the first company to provide unemployed people with training and support to be jointly owned by a County Council and the National Westminster Bank. He came to Scilly in 1991 and in January 1992 became the youngest chief executive in the country.

Housing is one of the issues that perplexes me most. Because the Government didn't see fit to exempt us from these laws, we have had to sell a significant proportion of council houses, but haven't had the right to develop our existing stock very much. This, set against the remarkably high cost of accommodation here, means that we do have a housing problem. Even with a head teacher's salary, it's difficult to find a mortgage and it is very difficult for young people to get on the housing ladder.

I think we were left out of the Water Privatization Act because water is a fundamental issue on the island. The system has worked well for a hundred years under the control of local government, and the community and Council were not prepared to see it taken away. Now we've been able to get a desalination plant which produces 50,000 gallons a day in the summer, and half that in the winter when the demand is less. It's the first permanently operating one in the UK.

The fact that a chief executive is a public figure in a small community was put to me in very forceful terms when I took over. I will be courteous and proper, but there are things I'm not prepared to discuss in the street, and I think people realized that very quickly. They see each other with remarkable frequency, but there's a respect for private life.

There is now the controversial issue as to whether we should introduce a landing tax or environmental levy to help cherish the environment, though the islands are protected by a range of statutory provision. It may be we can pursue National Park status which could bring in grants, but we must focus what we need to do before getting bogged down in the mechanism. I think the islands are of national importance in that they do restore people. I've seen visitors arriving, bowed down with the pressure of modern life, and then met them walking along the footpaths a week later, with a lot less care on their shoulders. It's a wonderful place for putting everything in perspective.

THE PHOTOGRAPHER

I am the fourth generation of photographers. My great-grandfather started in Scilly and I can trace one of his oldest photographs to 1869. By and large, I'm the only photographer here and I have to be able to do any job that comes up. Being in such an outlying place, there are obviously occasions when the London press can't get here and over the years we have managed one or two good news stories. In my father's day the BBC commentator Edward Ward came down to do a Christmas broadcast on the Bishop Rock Lighthouse. That's the last outpost here in the Atlantic. He thought he would be there three days, but it was six weeks before he could get off, and of course this poor man marooned with his engineer became world news. On the day the lifeboat eventually got him off, my father and I, went up in an aeroplane and he got that photograph spread over all the national papers. The time I got the most pictures used was when the helicopter tragically crashed between here and Penzance. Because it was such thick fog, all the aircraft were grounded and I was able to get the pictures of the six survivors as they came ashore.

Frank Gibson, sixty-four, was born on St Mary's, and his mother came from an old Scillonian family. His wife, Marie, helps with the administrative side of his business and they live in one of the first cottages to be built in Hugh Town in the early 1800s. They have three daughters and six grandchildren.

I produce the postcards for the islands – take the picture, publish it, and do the distribution myself and this is where my wife comes in handy because she looks after all the orders. I buy fifteen thousand postcards which will be cleared in three or four years and try to introduce a new picture every two years. Some standard sellers go on and on but because Scilly has so many regular visitors – some have been coming for over thirty years and are always looking for a new postcard – I have to keep producing them. I also do guidebooks, books on wild flowers, birds and anything which I think will sell in sufficient quantities.

My youngest daughter now lives in St Mary's with her husband (they run the Gibson-Kyne shop). I'd like them to take over what I've got because its a unique record of historical pictures. I've still got glass plates from my grandfather's time, my father's stuff and my own, so really it's a social documentary of Scilly. I do feel it's a record worth leaving.

THE BANK MANAGER

Peter Loxton, fifty-four, was born in Torquay and spent seven years in a North Cornwall bank, before coming to Scilly twenty-one years ago as Assistant Manager of Lloyds, one of two banks on the islands. In 1990 he became Branch Manager. He is a member of the 41 Club, is married to Phillippa, has one married daughter and one son, and is a grandfather.

The great advantage of being here is that I know most of my customers personally, and much about their background when they come to discuss various propositions. The disadvantages occur when you have to take strong action and when I visit off-islands at weekends, people sometimes don't hold back in coming up and discussing their banking business even though it's my day off. I do find it's necessary to go away from the islands for holidays.

These days, with the credit policy of the bank being one that isn't directed at taking risks, you do rely to some extent on the character and length of time our customers have been with us. We still have a village relationship here and I wouldn't want to change it. It seems to be the trend to get a second opinion on most things but my senior colleagues on the mainland rely on my length of experience here to a certain extent, and usually what I recommend stands.

Things have been pretty static over the last few years – I don't think there are many people wanting to come in from the mainland to buy up businesses as there were three or four years ago. I'm sure, too, that the price of fares must put some people off. I know some of my guest-house customers have said some people have phoned and agreed the tariff, then rung back later to say they'd have to cancel their booking because of the cost of getting here. If much of a reduction would change that, I don't know. But if it was a substantial one, neither of the transport operators would be able to afford to provide us with a service.

If anyone was planning to come over and start up a business, I'd always suggest they spend a month or two here during the winter. It is very different from the summer. Some who've come here on holiday think they'll have plenty of free time but find, once they've purchased their business, that they're working twenty-four hours a day in the summer, and when it comes to winter, and they have spare time, they're unable to enjoy the activities that drew them here.

Old Town Church across the bay,
St Mary's

Cottages in Hugh Street,
St Mary's

A view of Hugh Town, the islands'
only town, from the harbour

Bryher children come home by boat each
day from school on Tresco

Holiday-makers on St Mary's head for the
boats at the Old Quay and a day trip to the
island of their choice

The Neptune Steps, Tresco Abbey Gardens

The main road on Bryher with the white
garlic-smelling Three Cornered Leek
flowering beneath the stone wall

Blue Agapanthus in a cottage garden,
St Martin's

A view from the uninhabited island
of Samson

The St Agnes lighthouse, its tower
built in 1680, now a private dwelling

The Post Office and General Stores across the beach on Bryher with Tresco beyond

Gig racing, the most popular summer sport in Scilly

A beach on Tresco, one of hundreds of beautiful, unspoilt bays on the island

THE PILOT

There's compulsory pilotage round the islands for any vessel over 60 ft in length except Her Majesty's ships, and the main demand on a pilot these days is from cruise ships. We've had twenty-five in the summer months this year, which is a lot for Scilly. They average about 4,000 tons and 100 passengers, but occasionally you get a bigger one like the *Black Prince* with 400 to 500 people, and the *Maxim Gorki* with 1,500, who come mainly to see the Tresco gardens. We have a list of all the ships arriving during the year, though occasionally you get one out of the blue. In the last few years we've had several Blue Riband challenge attempts – Richard Branson's *Virgin Atlantic* and the biggest ever, the Aga Khan's *Destrierio*, which beat the Blue Riband record. It was bigger than the *Scillonian* and we were doing 65 knots when we came in.

John Nicholls, fifty-four, was born in Scilly and in 1956 went to sea as a Deck Officer Cadet in the Merchant Navy. He returned to Scilly ten years later, bought a 30 ft passenger launch and a 26 ft speedboat to take visitors round the islands. He is now the lifeboat's Hon. Sec. and with his wife, Mary, the owner of the 400-year-old Star Castle Hotel.

The pilot station is usually a couple of miles off Peninnis Head or the Bishop Lighthouse. I go out in the pilot boat *Surprise*, about half an hour before the ship is due in. It's mostly around 6 or 7 a.m. and I get up about 4.30 or 5 a.m. and give the ship a shout on the radio because it could be a long way off and behind time.

I know the waters well, but there's no one who knows it all. The man who says he does is not around. And the man who says he's happy in fog to me is not a good seaman, not honest with himself, because no one is happy in fog. You're relying on electronics which can fail you, and you do things with them today you wouldn't dare have done in years gone by. It's not so bad taking a ship out in fog because you're on board and acclimatized to the radar, but imagine getting off a bucking 30 ft boat, climbing the pilot ladder, going up about six flights of stairs, getting on a darkened bridge, and every radar is different. You could have a slight language problem and right away you're proceeding in confined waters. That sometimes is a little bit nerve racking, to say the least.

I'm also in charge of the lifeboat and responsible to the Institution at Poole. I'm called the Hon. Sec., but am the Launching Authority and if something happens, I am the one who gets the call from the coastguard and I have to decide whether the lifeboat goes or doesn't go. You obviously do this in conjunction with the coxswain and I wouldn't send it if he didn't want to go. But at three o'clock in the morning, when you get that call at your bedside, I've got to make a decision. In the summer the majority of jobs are picking up yachts with steering failure but a competent sailor should be able to make land without a rudder and the decision you often have to make is that you could be taking your lifeboat away from your own backdoor to go out 60 miles, and it's going to take three or four hours to get there. To tow it back at half the speed – you're talking about twelve hours away. Unless the weather is atrocious, the yacht should be able to make its own way back because you have to be very careful what you do with your lifeboat. God forbid I ever make a wrong decision.

The worst call I had was ten years ago when the BIH Sikorksy helicopter went down in the sea in thick fog. That's something that will always remain in my mind, one of the worst days of my life. It was a very sad day for Scilly, something that's always there.

THE FIREMAN

When there's a fire, we get the 999 system going through and we're all paged by paging units. The call comes through on the fax machine in the office, telling you where the fire is, and you pick it up as you come through the door. We also have radios we can talk to Cornwall with. We used to have a siren – well, we've still got it, funnily enough. It was the only form of calling us at one time. There was a button up at Telegraph Tower operated by the coastguards, but when we got the paging units, that was stopped. And there was a little bit of controversy over this – being a small community, everyone wants to know when there is a fire and with the pager units, they didn't. Councillors started saying, 'Why's the siren been taken off?' And I said, 'Well, it's this modern-day pager system, you don't need it any more.' So they

Kit Guy, fifty, the Station Officer of the Isles of Scilly Fire Brigade, is a Scillonian four generations back on both sides. He has a 70 acre flower farm, is married to a district nurse, with two children by his first marriage, four by his second. He has been in the fire brigade for about twenty-three years and is on call twenty-four hours a day.

reinstated it, and there it is on the wall. The first man through the door presses the button and the siren goes on for a minute. It's totally unnecessary, but if they want it and will pay for it being installed, then we use it.

We don't get a lot of fires – I'd say three-quarters of our calls are from yachtsmen, they drag their anchor, go on the rocks, have a hole in the boat. We normally put a pump aboard and get them back to St Mary's. We have about five or six shouts a year on that. In general, we get anything between forty and eighty calls a year. The worst fire was the Harbourside Hotel, the fridge overheated, caught alight, the kitchen and dining-room caught fire and it went right through and gutted it. The Scillonian Club caught alight once, a candle caught the curtain.

There are twelve members of the brigade – a schoolteacher, engineer, book-keeper, electrician, builder, hotelier, flower farmer and carpenter among them – and when we want any more, an ad is put in the Town Hall for recruits. What makes a good fireman? Teamwork. There is no one individual good fireman. If a man goes into a building, it's the man on the end of the pump that gives him water. If he stands out individually, he's no good to us. There are no heroes in the fire service, I'm afraid.

There are five firemen on each of the off-islands and they have a trailer towed by a tractor, except for Tresco where they have a Landrover. They carry about 200 gallons of water and various equipment. If there's a fire call, I'm notified and decide whether to send a crew over. My chief in Cornwall says we're never on our own over on Scilly, but we are, because it would be at least an hour and a half to two hours before he could get here. It's a responsibility, but that's what you take on and we try to get it right.

THE COUNCIL CHAIRMAN

The main grievance for our Authority is the mainland thinking which produces legislation inappropriate for the islands. But we have to conform and it seems unlikely we

Pat Greenlaw, sixty, from Birmingham, first visited Scilly in 1953 when he was in the Royal Navy. He came to live here in 1957, worked on a farm for a few months, and as an airport fireman for fourteen years. He stood for the Council in 1964, served for six years, resigned, and was re-elected eight years later. He is a painter and decorator and keen fisherman. He is married to Else, a former Land Girl on Tresco.

will be granted special consideration to meet our uniqueness. Every opportunity is taken to make this point but unfortunately with very little success. A lot of it comes down to common sense really. I personally don't like to see yellow lines all round the road, but there you are.

There are some drawbacks to not having party politics – we can't sit in groups and scrutinize issues before meetings. Apart from this, I think they're irrelevant for our Authority and when things aren't going a councillor's way, I tell them they have to remember that those who voted against them will probably be on their side at the next meeting.

Sometimes when I make a decision, it's not so easy the next day – local people want to know in greater detail why I've made it – you can't avoid that and it keeps you on your toes, which is good. I've always found the best way of dealing with a controversial issue is to meet people and give them the opportunity to put their viewpoint. They respect that there are occasions when we will disagree, but generally speaking, they don't get personal about it. That's something I try to avoid.

Big issues? Whether there should be more development is something we'll have to spend a lot of time on. And the coast erosion. The only way to get grants for this is to have reports from experts, but when they say £18 million is required, councillors ask why we're going down that road. Housing for young local people is a continuing issue – we're frequently told to provide more houses, but how much development can the Isles of Scilly stand? There must be a limit. My feeling is that the attractiveness of the islands lies in what they are now and if they're developed any more, they would lose this and our economy would suffer. But it's easy for me to say that because I have a roof over my head.

What I want to bring about is discussions with young islanders about their future. They must have an input into this important issue. If they wish to see further development, they must understand the consequences – more sewers, more traffic, for example. It's not good enough for the likes of me and colleagues of my age to start laying down the laws for them. What's interesting is that when a group of islanders are talking together and you say, 'What about traffic?', they say, 'There's far too much.' 'What about development?' 'Oh no, no more.' But when you get down to the individual, they don't come out with the same thinking. They say it's their right to have this or that.

One of the community's main concerns at present is the cost of travel to the islands. We've looked at some kind of government subsidy which the Scottish islands get, but this would require local operators to produce facts and figures to substantiate such a claim. The Steamship Company, which has served the islands for many years, are having a difficult time – the recession is really biting here now – but we must have a vessel running back and forth and if we have to lose anything, it shouldn't be a ship. The company gets a lot of criticism and I'm party to it from time to time. It's not deserved in many places, but they do seem to find great difficulty in relating to the community on many things.

THE MIDWIFE AND STAFF NURSE

There are four midwives and we do need that number to give a twenty-four hour coverage. One mother has had all her children on an off-island, but it's not something we encourage because of the lack of facilities in case anything should go wrong. Some years ago, they would have had to come to St Mary's two weeks before, but because transport is much better, unless the weather is really bad, they only come across when they're in labour. They ring us up and the medical launch will go and pick them up. The worst island to get to is St Agnes, but Rodney Terry, the medical launch boatman, hasn't had a birth aboard yet though there was one lady who I thought had lots of time, then she rang when the boatman was on his way, to say things were happening very fast. But all was well. Rodney has had a lot of experience at sea, and you really feel very secure with him taking them off.

Margaret Bourdeaux, forty-seven, studied general nursing at St Mary Abbotts, Kensington and midwifery at Dartford, Kent and came to work in Scilly in 1969. She is married to John, the potter, and they have two children.

It's very different being a midwife here than on the mainland. We know the person before they're pregnant, we may have delivered *them*, and we see them all the time throughout the pregnancy. They seem to do so much better when they come into labour than mothers on the mainland. They're very relaxed, seem to take a shorter time and need less pain-killing drugs.

If there's any abnormality, off they go to the mainland. A colleague had a very hard decision to make recently. A mother was not progressing in labour and the fog was coming in and she had to decide whether to transfer the mother to the mainland or wait and see how things went. She decided to err on the side of caution, called the RNAS Culdrose (Royal Naval Air Services) emergency helicopter service, and she and the doctor went off with the mother. They were touching down on the mainland when the mother decided that was the time for the baby to be born and she had it there and then in the helicopter. Our midwifery supervisor said to my colleague afterwards, 'I hope you assured the patient's privacy at all times.' And she said, 'I did my best.'

Husbands seem very much at home in the hospital. I suppose it doesn't feel like one. There's usually only one person in labour at once, so the midwife will be there for the whole time and the mother can stay in as long as she likes. Some stay for the full ten days, others prefer to go home after two or three. Then we become a community nurse and visit them daily. I think they feel very cared for. After ten days they're handed over to the health visitor.

The hospital has thirteen beds, two are midwifery and used exclusively for that. The rest could be anything. If we have a lot of women in, we'll put them in the bigger male ward and that will become the female ward! Then we have a three-bedded ward which is for the care of the elderly. Everything is interchangeable. At the moment we're building a little suite for terminally ill patients, to be like a hospice, which will have a room for the patient with a really beautiful view over the sea to St Agnes, en suite facilities, and a bed-sitting room for relations to stay.

On the nursing front, we never know what will come through the door, and we have to deal with everything. Visitors are the ones who have the most injuries, fractured wrists and ankles. They're walking around on the rocks, jumping on to boats and things they'd never do otherwise. We have injured fishermen too.

It can be difficult being in a place where you are so known. People will stop you in the Co-op and ask about an in-patient. Sometimes you have to be rude because you can't give diagnoses of patients in the Co-op. But I do find it very nice to know people and look after them and their families. The difficult part is getting attached to patients who are terminally ill. When a long-term patient dies, you come in on the morning and their room is empty and that's really bad. We've known them before they've come in, had treatment, and are out in the community again. But we do manage to live again, and be ready for the next person.

THE WELL-PERSON NURSE

We have a Health Promotion Clinic for men and women and call people regularly about every three years. We do basic measurements of weight and blood pressure and cervical cytology for women, and talk about smoking, alcohol, diet, exercise and stress. This year we're going to extend our Well Persons Clinic down to the fifteen-year-olds.

I know what most people's work is and this does help. For instance, it's not much good making appointments for the boatmen to come in the middle of the summer because they're busy, and it's no good asking flower farmers in the flower season. Hoteliers and guest-house owners are more accessible on a summer afternoon than in the winter when they're doing conversions or are away. We get about an 80 per cent uptake and I'm now on to the second and third recall. More come than they used to, with more women

Liz Ellis, fifty, came to Tresco in 1961 to work in the quay shop before starting nursing at Guy's Hospital. She did midwifery in Plymouth and worked on the district in Penzance and St Ives. In 1965 she came to Scilly as a staff-nurse midwife and married a Scillonian in 1970. She was a district nurse for fourteen years.

57

than men – the women are very keen on their cytology even though they know they have to suffer a nag about their weight. It's more difficult to get people from the off-islands but it's better for them to come here than me go to them. The surgeries on there are very basic.

There are some subjects I suggest men talk to the doctor about, but I'm surprised how freely they do talk to me. Perhaps it's better the devil they know. There are quite a few with alcohol problems and we like to suggest that they should be aware of what is a reasonable level. We have an alcohol councillor and when there was talk about her coming, the doctor asked if I could draw up a list of anyone who I thought might be a candidate and I drew up about forty names without thinking too hard. Probably more men than women.

I don't know the reason for this. People say it's lack of other things to do, which isn't true. The pub *is* a social meeting-place, and maybe it goes on from there. I'm surprised how much off-islanders drink at home, especially in the flower season. They treat it as medicinal after a cold day out picking flowers. It's OK as long as it's for a short time.

We're also trying to promote mental health. Stress management is the in-phrase at the moment, recognizing it and dealing with it. Being in business is always stressful but the good thing here is that people often have several irons in the fire and if the husband's job is not doing too well, the wife's can be alright. Professional people are a bit isolated – there's no equivalent person in many cases to chew things over with and they never get away from the job.

THE DOG WARDEN

Being a dog warden is a part-time job and I do fifteen hours a week. But I'm on call all the time and people will ring up from six in the morning until 10.30 at night telling me there's a dog on the beach, because they're not allowed to be there.

It all started when I was walking over from Old Town one day and saw someone letting their dog foul on the pavement. I was absolutely furious, went up to him and said, 'Look, do you think that is a nice thing to do?' And he said, 'I don't care, no one can fine me, there isn't a dog warden here.' So I went straight round to the Town Hall and said, 'I believe you haven't got a dog warden.' And they said, 'No.' And I said, 'Well, I'll apply for the job', and they said, 'You've got it.'

Then I started to wonder what on earth I'd taken on. There are upwards of about two hundred dogs on the island and they're all very good, it's just the owners that are a bit naughty. We have by-laws banning dogs from Porth Mellon, Porthcressa and Old Town beaches from 30 April to 30 September, national laws by which it's an offence for dogs to foul pavements, and local by-laws which prevent them messing on some areas of grass. But it's awfully difficult to catch them at it. You get there just after or before the offence has been committed.

There haven't been any convictions at all yet – I try to avoid them if I can. But if people persistently allow their dogs to foul, then we'll have to do something. When I have caught dogs at it, I tell the owner to clean it up, and they say, 'Why?' and I tell them it's the law. So far they always have cleaned it up, which stops the law coming into force. The Town Hall and the Environmental Trust give out poop scoops so there's no excuse not to have one. I'm not talking about visitors here. I find they are generally much better than locals, who let their dog out in the morning and know it will come back some time later in the evening. What it's doing during the day doesn't seem to matter to them at all.

We haven't got proper kennels here. We've got a rabies pen but I wouldn't put a dog in there, because I wouldn't do that to my worst enemy. It's just a cage. I'm now lobbying councillors to get some kind of kennelling started. People like to bring their dogs on holiday and want to kennel them out if hotels won't take them. The local authority could also use kennels to house stray dogs as the need does arise from time to time.

I'm glad if my job is doing some good, but I don't enjoy it. There's nothing to enjoy particularly. It's a job you have

Thirty-two-year-old Julia Miles' grandparents came to St Agnes just before the war and her parents just after it. She works as a receptionist at the Tregarthen Hotel, was a gig racer for nine years and became the islands' dog warden in 1991. She is married and has one son.

to take quite seriously and I'm not a terribly serious-minded person. But I was determined to do something about it, and I think I have.

THE UNDERWATER SAFARI TEACHER

Mark Groves, forty, was born on St Mary's and has lived in 'Nowhere', the name of his house in Old Town, for thirty-nine years. He was with VSO in Botswana for a year, took a degree in geology at Portsmouth College, worked as a geologist in Saudi Arabia, and as a diver in the Red Sea. In 1984 he started Underwater Safaris.

I don't teach people to dive – just give them the experience of going under water. They should be able to swim, but I've taken some who can't. Not many, and they usually tell you afterwards! In May the water is about 11°, in January and February about 8° or 9°. In the summer it varies a lot – the deep water is about 13° or 14°, off the beaches it can go up to 18°.

I've taken all ages and abilities from as young as seven, but that's unusual. About ten or eleven is the average youngest and size is the important factor. A big ten-year-old is OK, but if the tank they wear on their back is too long, it sticks in the back of their neck. The oldest person was eighty-four, and he came back for a second go. I've had a couple propose to each other under water. I had to get an under-water slate and a pencil and he wrote 'Will you marry me?' and she wrote 'Yes'. And now they're happily married.

The marine life here is about the best in the British Isles. We don't have pollution in the water and we're far enough south to get quite a few Mediterranean species. On the east coast of England, visibility is nil and 'very good' would be a few feet. Here it would be 40, 50 or even 100 ft.

People have looked at my book on marine life and said, 'You've got a bit of a cheek selling this book – these photographs weren't taken here.' They couldn't believe they were. I give a weekly slide show with colour pictures of the anemones, fish and sea urchins and because people never see underwater films about the British Isles, they don't think there's a bloody thing here. But we have quite strong tides, and on the extremities of the islands, the rocks go straight down a 100 ft, a sheer wall covered with marine life.

I've only found one interesting wreck – it was one of four that sank on 22 October 1707 and over two thousand men were lost. Three of the wrecks were found in the 1960s – *The Association*, *The Eagle*, and the *Romney*. I found the fourth in 1981 – it was *The Firebrand*, which sank at the back of St Agnes. It was quite a small ship, about 75 ft long, with forty-five men on board of which twenty-six survived. Finding it was very exciting. It was right at the end of the dive, and I'd been drift diving for well over half a mile and was just about to come up. Then I saw something in the distance. I went over to have a look and there were two very large anchors. I looked around and could see these cannons. Then your heart starts going, you've heard all these stories of treasure chests. And then I saw more anchors and more cannons. By this time I was getting very low on air so I stuck the anchor in and was just going back to the boat when I happened to look under the cannon, and there was the ship's bell. And then my air ran out, so I had to come to the surface. We lifted the bell the next day and it had 1692 on it. It's now in a Penzance museum, but the actual thrill of finding it was wonderful and I'll never forget it. We've just kept the ship as it is for new divers to go and see what an old wreck site looks like.

THE EDITOR

The reason for starting *Scilly up to Date* was because we thought it would be good to bring opinion about controversial things into the open. There were Council meetings but you couldn't speak there, and one had this feeling things weren't properly discussed. There is *The Scillonian* magazine, but it's only published twice a year. So we talked to John Read the printer, and I told him I didn't want to make money out of it, and we started with 16 pages and 1,000 copies. We now have 44 pages and publish 6,500 copies. Tourists can order it and only pay postage and packing and I ask them to give some money to an island

Gunnar Schweer, seventy-two, was born in Germany and worked as a journalist before the Second World War during which he was sent to a prisoner of war camp in Leicester. After visiting Scilly on holiday, and disliking the political climate in Germany, he and his wife, Usch, decided to settle here. He has written two books about Hamburg, and in 1985 launched *Scilly up to Date*, which is now published nine times a year.

charity of their own choice. As well as giving people a place to air their feelings, its purpose is also to inform holiday guests and locals of island events. Normally we limit entries to Scillonian topics, though I can't help going into politics, but I try to be a little ironic. I also tend to take sides, but we do have a letter section where people can say what they like, too. There's a tendency for them to write poems and I must admit I can't see any sense in them.

The first big controversial issue was the rubbish tip. The Council wanted to use a quarry which we said was not big enough and would pollute the water which would then seep into the sea where people bathe. Then there was the airport runway extension controversy; and the bottle bank – there was only one outside the Town Hall and after two days it was full so the Steamship Company transported it to the mainland. So there wasn't one here until it was brought back. Then the Council had to employ a workforce to put the bottles lying on the ground back in the bank and then it was full again!

Generally we have been made very welcome, and this is home now, though I still enjoy going to Hamburg. Usch is an organic gardener and knows every earthworm personally. When there is a tour bus full of Germans and the driver is not sure if they will understand his English, I go along as interpreter. I sometimes have phone calls from the BBC in Plymouth wanting to know if there is anything juicy going on. I try to avoid writing things which are not of importance and which are hurtful to people. We had one story here which hit the nationals and I had phone calls from the tabloids in London who wanted photos of the people involved. But I refused, and no one else in the island was ready to give them either. We ignored it in *Scilly up to Date* too.

There are some rather Conservative farmers here and one of them once approached me and said, 'You are very Left' which isn't really the case. But quite a lot of mainland issues could affect Scilly – privatizing the post office, the water, and the prisons – I did a piece about offering glossy brochures to people who are convicted so they can choose which prison to go to. Some don't appreciate my humour. But once I was rather fed up and saying I was looking for somebody to take over the paper, and quite a lot of people said, 'Oh, you must carry on, we like you to do it, and you do it very well.'

THE ENTREPRENEUR

We'd been coming to Scilly for twenty-five years, so we had an idea what we were coming to, but it's probably taken us five years to adjust. When you first come, it's very colourful, you breathe in all the fresh air, but you get pangs of claustrophobia. You need to go back and see the shops and the people, and if you have a family, you feel a little way away from them. Life here is all about the sea, all about boats and there were times when I wanted to catch up with the foreign exchange rate, see what was going on in California where I used to commute to. I had withdrawal symptoms and wanted to go back, but it wasn't possible because I'd made the decision not to carry on with the rat race I'd been in. Now I feel a part of the islands and can happily say we wouldn't go back to the mainland.

George Teideman, fifty-one, was the managing director of a multi-national optics pharmaceutical company which six years ago sent him to Australia. When his wife, Margaret, said she wouldn't live there, he left the company, came to Scilly and bought a restaurant. A year later, he sold it and bought the Atlantic Hotel. He produces a monthly programme about Scilly for BBC Radio Cornwall and has made a tape, 'Scilly by George' to raise money for the RNIB.

I'm a hotel proprietor, but I like to think of myself more as an entrepreneur, a public relations man. When groups of people come to the hotel, we say, 'Sit down. If you're interested, we'll tell you something about what it's like to live here, what makes an islander, what makes him tick.' I tell them how islanders lived in the past and the industries that were here. Each day has a different theme and I take them round the off-islands. In the evening we put on events like visiting a local artist or potter.

The price of travelling here is ridiculously expensive. I sympathize with the operators – to run a helicopter isn't a cheap business – but somewhere along the line we've got to find a cheaper way. In the old days people used to come for a day trip on the boat. The price was relatively acceptable and they'd think, this is fantastic, we're coming back to see the place properly next year. But because of the high fares, they don't come anyway, so we're losing out in terms of next year's business.

I know we have to work quite hard to get people to come here, but I don't think we're nearly aggressive enough. My angle is: it costs a lot of money to come, but that's alright because when you get here, you'll think it's absolutely worth it.

THE GOLF STEWARD

Liz Heslin, forty-four, came to Scilly when her father was postmaster. She ran the Atlantic bars for two years, had a small restaurant, managed holiday flats, and a guest-house. Last year she opened a ladies clothes shop with a friend, and was recently appointed steward at the Golf Club. She is separated from her husband and has two children and a grandson.

It's a beautiful golf-course right over the sea. Come up on a sunny day and walk around – it must have one of the best views in the country. We've only got nine holes, but eighteen tees. We need more members, the green is very expensive to keep up though Peter Stringer, the greenkeeper, does a fantastic job. I was surprised to get the job – a woman on her own. I'm the first woman to be steward in eighty years. But they knew I'd done catering and I think it was better the devil they knew.

I get up at six, sit out on the balcony and have a cup of tea. It's so peaceful and beautiful looking out on to the harbour and the islands, they're different every day. There's all-day food; Monday evening there's Rotary; Tuesday, the 41 Club; Wednesday, golfers. It's a members only club at night, unless you're invited, but I'd like to have more people come in. It's not snobby at all. We have lots of young players in their twenties, builders, chefs, waiters, shopkeepers, and a lot of boatmen. We had a dinner last night – farmers and boatmen, they have three or four matches during the summer. The boatmen are really into golf now. On the mainland, you have to have money to play and some of the fees are dreadful. Here I think it's about £160 a year for full membership, holiday-makers pay £14 a day.

There are definitely more men than women. They don't like women on the course [laughs]. Chauvinism, I suppose. I said the other week, 'I'm going to take up golf in November.' Being a steward I felt I should at least have some idea of what it's all about. And one of the lads said, 'Oh, no, not another woman!' I said what's wrong with women on the course? The young girl who works for me, she's just finished university and is going to take it up as well, so the two of us will go out together when there's nobody else around.

We had a ten-piece band about two weeks ago which caused a bit of, what shall I say, excitement? I was told they wanted the club built up a bit with a few more functions. Members don't have to wear ties, but they're meant to be smart casual, so I asked the captain if the group could play as they were, you couldn't very well ask them to put suits on, and he said we should go ahead. Members were apprehensive when they saw the band coming in – one of the girls had striped leggings, shorts, a crew cut, and a stud in her nose. A lovely woman, her husband's an architect. But it was a brilliant evening, everyone danced and I'm hoping we'll be able to have the group back again.

In 1928 the Isles of Scilly Golf Club had the first lady captain in the UK.

THE COASTGUARD

I became a coastguard when we had six or seven regular coastguard officers and a watch was kept twenty-four hours a day. We've now only got one regular full-time officer, and each island has an auxiliary in charge with the rest of us auxiliaries who make up the total number required.

When you're in the coastguard tower, you're listening to the radio and keeping a radio watch. We keep a visual watch as well if it's not foggy, in case there are any flares or distress signals. If there's a red or smoke flare, the immediate response is to bang off two white flares from the tower, so the person who has sent it knows someone has seen it and they can think, 'Oh thank God for that, something's going to happen soon.' We then phone Falmouth, which is our controlling station, and tell them

Rosemary Codd, forty-nine, was born on Tresco, moved to Bryher and left the islands with her family when she was eight. She worked in a veterinary practice, got married, had two children, and returned to Scilly twenty years ago. She has since been divorced and remarried.

65

what's happened and where. I think the communication side is very important. If people are having a bad time, or they're frightened, knowing someone is there on the shore and ready to help if it really gets bad can give them the freedom to actually get on and do something about the situation.

There are two women in our group and, in my opinion, I think Alan, our boss, thinks this is quite enough! Not because it's sexist but because when you get a yacht stranded, he'd rather have men with strength to go out with lines, who've known, since the year dot, how to handle a boat, and know what to do instinctively. I'm not saying women can't do this, and in some stations they do. But we do have other uses: we can operate searchlights, man the radio. Men love to be out and some get bored out of their minds sitting up the coastguard tower for six hours doing a routine watch.

On watch, you can read as long as you look up as often as you can and don't get totally into the book and forget what's going on. I think it's absolutely wonderful to have six hours in total seclusion and isolation.

THE METHODIST MINISTER

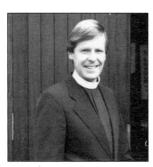

Jeremy Dare, forty-one, was born in Bexhill on Sea, Sussex. An engineer by trade, he 'changed courses', trained at the Methodist Theological College in Bristol and spent five years in south London before coming to Scilly six years ago. He is Chairman of the Senior School's Governors, married to Jill and they have a daughter, Marianne, seven.

We were quite concerned about coming here as neither my wife nor I had ever lived anywhere with less than several tens of thousands of people, and we didn't know how the island culture would accept us. It's lovely to be able to leave the church open without having to be there and there are now seventy-eight people on our membership roll. We've found a lot of our members come from the Salvation Army and the Baptists because we are the Free Church, and this creates interesting hopes for what we might do in the future. We have some services with the Anglican church, not as many as we could but, with the present incumbent, a lot more than we did.

A typical day? I do one or more lessons at the senior school or take an assembly and most days will include a visit to the hospital or old peoples' home. Visitors to Scilly have accidents, strokes or heart attacks, and they can be a bit lonely away from their family and friends. There's usually something on every evening – a slide show about Scilly, a committee meeting, a concert. I sometimes go to the garage and do a bit of lathe work – I think it makes it easier for people to talk if I'm doing something else. We're like the shopkeepers and the boatmen – different visitors have anchor people whom they tie a rope round when they come to pitch their holiday tent.

At least one morning a week I'll spend two hours going down to the post office, and a lot of people come and talk about things that are important to them. It makes contacts on behalf of the church and I feel it's useful just to be around. It's where I pick up most of my information about anyone who is ill or has an anniversary. It's useful to hear about these things and be able to respond. It's just . . . being available.

THE RECTOR

I have six churches to look after – two on St Mary's and one on each of the other inhabited islands. Every day at 5 p.m. there is Evensong at the parish church and in the summer on Sunday, there's the Epilogue in the little church at Old Town. If you want to get a flavour of what people, perhaps, take away from Scilly, you should go to this church. It's right on the edge of the beach, the service is by candlelight and there's a very special atmosphere. I think it's due to the fact that prayer has been offered on this spot for over a thousand years.

The four off-island churches each have a service every week in the summer but from October to March, they're on a rota basis: once a month for St Agnes, Bryher and St Martin's, twice for Tresco. The parish has a non-stipendiary curate, Father Keith Campion, who also works in a secular job, and Mrs Pam Millyard, a Parish Reader. The percentage of the island population going to church is ten times the national average for church going in this country, so percentage-wise, it's very high. And if you look at it like that, it gives you heart to go trudging to the off-islands in the rain in the middle of winter.

On the Sunday nearest to 8 August every summer, there's

Father Michael Phillips, thirty-nine, took a degree in law at Trent Polytechnic, Nottingham, worked in the Probation Service, went to a theological college in Salisbury and was ordained. He became chaplain in a maximum security prison and an English-speaking church in Hong Kong, and rector in Tokyo of the only English-speaking diocesan church in Japan. He came to Scilly in 1991, is married to Rae, and they have three children.

a pilgrimage to the uninhabited island of St Helen's where a hermit called St Elidius once lived and is buried. We all go off in boats, clamber up the beach and have a service in the ruins of the shrine. It was in AD 993 that Olaf Tryggvesson, later King of Norway, came to see the shrine and was converted to Christianity. The following year, a Peace Treaty was drawn up between Olaf and Ethelred the Unready, and as a result of Olaf's conversion here in Scilly, Scandinavia became Christian. It shows how one man or a tiny community in a far-off place can actually affect the rest of the world.

About 60 per cent of the population here are Methodist and there's a Roman Catholic chapel which doesn't have a priest. But last year Mrs Millyard's husband, Michael, was appointed the Eucharistic Minister, and now the RC parish priest comes over about four times a year from Penzance to consecrate the bread which Michael administers.

I think the main social problem here is the number of marital break-downs, which seems higher than on the mainland. I was talking to a Scillonian about this and he said he thought it was because if you live in the middle of London, walk down the street and see a pretty girl, you never see her again. Here, you go into the post office, there's the pretty girl and three days later you may see her again. The geography of the place forces people together and because of the price of fares to the mainland – to get my family to Penzance, for example, costs about £260 – people rarely go away, and sometimes in a relationship you do need a bit of space. It may seem strange to say this when you have beautiful deserted beaches around you, but there is nowhere you can go where someone doesn't know you. Privacy can be a problem.

THE FISHERMEN

Martin Bond: Today I got up at 4.45 a.m., and now at 7 p.m. I haven't quite finished work yet. But tomorrow it's probably going to blow a gale, so I'll suit myself and do a few jobs on land. I fish for lobsters and crawfish mainly. I leave home at 6 a.m. and if I'm only doing lobster pots, I can be home by lunch-time. If I've got nets to do as well, then I go on and on. My nets are 400 yd long and if I get eight or ten fish in them, I'm quite happy. The majority goes to the Continent – I don't know why more aren't taken here. You never see crawfish in English restaurants, except perhaps on the Cornish coast or in Wales, but the Spanish and French love it.

Martin Bond, forty-one, was born in Scilly, went into the Merchant Navy, worked as a fisherman on St Martin's but, with nowhere to live, returned to the Merchant Navy. In 1980 he settled in St Mary's. He is in the lifeboat service, married to Lorraine 'Skinny', the post lady, and they have three children.

In the afternoon, I make new nets, patch holes, the boat has to be kept running. In the evening I go sailing with my son. The only thing that governs you here is the elements and apart from that nobody can tell you what to do. I don't socialize much except for standing on the slipway and gossiping on a windy day.

There's a higher level of fishing now than ever – having a licence doesn't solve anything. There's a 3 mile limit round the islands and you can't fish inside it if your boat is over 36 ft long or is registered more than 10 tons which helps a bit, but it would help more if the limit was taken to 6 miles. It's a big worry because you have so much pressure from boats outside. The Spanish, French and Belgians are out there in their hundreds, most are breaking the law but the authorities can't stop them. The Fishing Protection patrols keep an eye on them, but they're rather infrequent.

You have to try and fish as sensibly as you can to preserve the stock but it's hard because you have to make x amount of money to be viable. Some people don't care, they fish as if there was no tomorrow, but I like to think most of us take a long-term view. One of the worst crimes in my book is bringing ashore undersize immature fish. A lobster is seven years old before it's big enough to be caught but some fishermen haven't got the sense to know that if they throw a young lobster back, it will be half as big again next year. Below the minimum size (the shell on the back has to be 90 cm), they haven't even had a chance to breed.

Tim Short: I came back to Scilly because of my children – I wanted to educate them here. I had no idea what I would do but I've always enjoyed pulling lobster pots, and this is what I've ended up doing.

Life is now a wonderful arrangement. I start one day at 5 a.m. and the next day it's 6 a.m. because I have to work at low tide. Every day it gets an hour later. I have a 30 ft fairly fast fishing boat, and fish at a group of rocks, a rather awesome place, called the Sevenstones, a third of the way to Land's End. Most people here with small boats my size work on their own, but the rocks I go to are particularly unpleasant and you really need two people. But because no one else goes, there are more lobsters so that pays for the second man. Once a week, we send them away to the mainland – all the hotels here are covered by the boys who've been doing it for thirty or forty years and I don't want to tread on anyone's toes. Lobsters are pretty much all the year round, but the weather gets so bad in winter that only one gentleman keeps going. The rest of the potting boats pack it in October/November time and start again in March.

For the last two years in winter I've taken a boat from France and delivered it in the Caribbean. It's wonderful, it gets warmer every day, almost too good to be true, though I'm not sure how much my wife approves of me disappearing for two months each winter.

I have to have a definite purpose to a job, and I thoroughly enjoy what I'm doing now in Scilly. If the weather's nice in the morning, it's like something out of a picture book – the sun's just getting up, the islands look beautiful. And when its windy and miserable, it's quite exciting. But when it's thick fog, or there's a lot of wind, you really do wonder what you're doing out there. And then I think what else would I be doing, and there's no other option that is as attractive.

Tim Short, fifty-one, was born on Scilly, trained to be a teacher, worked at the Central College of Physical Recreation at Crystal Palace, at an Outward Bound school in Wales, built a boat and sailed away to Barbados. He went for a year and stayed twenty, married Buffa, an American, and they have two young daughters.

THE TOURISM OFFICER

Having different jobs raises eyebrows on the mainland but here it's an accepted fact – you can be a dustman one day, assistant chief executive the next. Well, not quite the next, but it's been a steady progression.

Tourism is now worth an annual £30m to the islands, 85 per cent of their revenue, and the tourism team has developed quite dramatically over the last five or six years. Last year our net budget was £49,100 but we spent something in the region of £95,000 as the income from some of our ventures has got greater. From selling a small number of guidebooks and maps, we now have a full-blown *Isles of Scilly Guide* and for the first time ever, the Council was persuaded to include advertising in it – it made something like a £20,000 profit. We produce a mini-guide in French, German and English, a new day visitors' leaflet, a weekly 'What's On' publication and operate a computerized vacancy service.

We estimate we have around three and a half thousand bed spaces which includes camp sites, self-catering accommodation, hotels, guest-houses and the non-registered places that do B&B on an occasional basis. The most visitors we've had in the last five years between April and October has been about 126,000, which includes day visitors as well as stayers. Last year we were down to about 87,000 which is the lowest since 1981 when I think it was about 85,000. Over the last twenty years 100,000 has been a good average. Perhaps the fact that we haven't got more accommodation, or the transport to bring more people in, is a useful blessing – we can't be overrun.

Most tourists come from Britain, then Germany, an increasing number from America, and yachts from France. I think ignorance about where Scilly is, is slowly declining, though one travel agent came up to me and said he wanted everything I'd got on Italy, because he thought we were Sicily. And that was a travel agent! I think visitors from the UK mainland do feel they're coming abroad. With our white beaches, it's not difficult to imagine you're in the

Steve Watt, fifty, was born on Scilly, but brought up on the mainland. On returning to the islands, he was a dustman for seven years, then took a three year teacher training course followed by a year's study at Exeter University where he gained a degree. He taught on the mainland for ten years before returning to Scilly where he fished and farmed until, in 1988, he became the islands' first Tourism Officer. He is also Assistant Chief Executive of the Isles of Scilly Council, and Secretary of the golf club, is married and has two children.

Caribbean, apart from the sea temperature which, at 12° to 13°, is a bit nippy. Many believe the Gulf Stream goes round the islands. It doesn't. It's about 200 miles to the west, but we are affected by the weather patterns which come up on it, so very often when there's a huge high pressure over the Azores, we get the top end of it whereas England doesn't. Late afternoon in the spring tide when the sea's coming in on top of hot sand, it can be extremely warm in scores of our secluded bays.

People here are very nationalistic but only about the islands. We regard England as a small island, east-north-east of Scilly. We're not really Cornish, though if it came to a fight and it was Cornwall versus the rest, we know which side we'd be on. We're a separate kingdom – we're Scillonians.

THE PHARMACIST

Chris Douglas, fifty-three, a member of the Royal Pharmaceutical Society, moved to Scilly with his family in pre-National Health 1945 when his father was offered a senior partnership in the local pharmacy. He studied pharmacy at Portsmouth College of Technology where he met his wife, Judy, a pharmacist, and they have three children. He is a school governor and a Trustee of the Environmental Trust.

This is the only pharmacy in the islands. We're not contracted to the NHS, but I work in conjunction with the doctor at the Health Centre. If there's an emergency on the off-islands, a prescription can arrive here and be back with them the same evening, or in winter perhaps the next day. In the summer, if they have a sore throat or bronchitis, the doctor will want them to come to St Mary's to see him. You have to time being ill correctly if you live on an off-island!

We have quite a good stock in the shop, but some visitors get quite aggrieved because we haven't got the specific size or flavour of indigestion tablets they usually have. It's funny what their perceptions of the islands are. Saturday afternoon, they'll bring you a prescription which they've had for about three weeks, for the most remote sort of product, and express horror if we haven't actually got it in stock, and that it might take two days to come. But if there was no holiday industry, there'd be no pharmacy.

In good weather, you can predict visitors will come in with ultraviolet induced rashes. People get burnt here because they associate being burnt with high temperatures which we don't have, rather than the ultraviolet which is much stronger here than you might get anywhere else north of the Equator. They won't get as burnt in the Mediterranean where the temperature is in the 80s, as they will here on a bright clear day.

THE ARTIST

I work fairly fast, I work hard. I'm what they call an accurate painter, a traditional painter. I work a lot from photographs although I must take them myself and I must know the area quite well. I quite enjoy painting with people around me. The pictures that are difficult to start, I do in the early morning, so from seven to nine I have complete peace and quiet. As well as the oils, I also do a lot of prints of Scilly because people love to take something back that reminds them of the islands, and they can have a small print, a pack of cards or place mats, without spending a great deal.

I tend to say to people, 'If you love this painting, you have it, and I'm sure you'll pay for it one day.' What happens is that it burns a hole on their wall until it's paid for. And it does get paid for very quickly. Anyone who buys a painting of the Scillies from me and loves the Scillies will not do anything they shouldn't do. One of the great joys of the islands is that it is a trusting, friendly place, one of the very few left in Britain. And the people of St Mary's are some of the nicest people in the world. Every community has its problems, but unless you want to be terribly politically minded and just want to live at peace with your neighbours, you couldn't come to a nicer place.

Sadly, John Hamilton died suddenly at the end of December 1993.

John Hamilton, seventy-four, served in the Army, worked in the Borstal service in Britain and Ghana and was deputy group personnel manager of the Reed Paper Group before settling on Tresco. He started a community jewellery-making business, but had to give it up through illness. He taught himself to draw and paint, and produced a history of the Second World War at sea in eighty-four paintings which, in 1977, were exhibited at the Guildhall, London, before being bought and presented to the Imperial War Museum. His 120 paintings of the war in the Pacific hang in the Pentagon, Washington. His books include *War at Sea, The Helicopter Story of the Falklands War* and *Sketching with a Pencil for those who are just Beginning.* He is Secretary of the UK Antarctic Heritage Trust, has been an Isles of Scilly councillor, is married to Betty, and has two grown-up children.

THE POTTER

John Bourdeaux, forty-eight, was brought to Scilly every year from the time he was born to when he was ten and in 1969 his family settled here permanently. He worked for four years as a marketing trainee in Harrods before returning to Scilly to be a potter. He is married to Margaret, a midwife, and they have two sons. In 1993 he became a local councillor.

I make about a thousand different lines, a lot of hand-thrown and neo-modernist work, and use lots of local minerals for glazes – granite, copper, manganese and iron. I pick up all sorts of things and see what happens. I think the only thing I stipulate is that my pottery has got to be different from anyone else's and, as I've no idea what I'm going to do next, it's always quite exciting. A range of life-size sea birds has gone all over the world.

I work on my own and it is very, very enjoyable. I could have got bigger and I've turned down many commissions to stay happy. There was a big flower arranging firm who wanted two thousand items at a time, but I didn't even think about it. I didn't want to ruin my nice way of life, which it would have done, without a doubt. And I wouldn't have been able to stop and chat to visitors, as I do. That's the whole point of being here really, the social side as much as the pottery. I've got people who've come for seventeen years, ever since the pottery's been open, and they collect something different every time and take a bit of Scilly back with them in the pots. I think these typify Scilly – they're a bit dusty and rugged, not posh. If you can make someone smile with a bit of mug, you're beginning to win.

THE HAIRDRESSER

There are two salons here in St Mary's and we work very well together. If I'm busy, I'll send customers down to Jane and she'll do the same for me. We've got our local clientele and some float around, but there's never any argument because when you're living on an island, you've got to do a lot of giving and taking. It can get very silly if you try to outdo the other one.

Both salons are unisex, but I think most of the local men get their hair cut by their wives – that's why there isn't a barber. It's probably just the life-style – they haven't got to look like city gents. We keep quite up to date though and quite trendy because we get all the hotel staff from the cities with their new haircuts, and have to keep them going. Old people from the rest home come down in their bus for their perms and trims, and sometimes I go to the hospital to do people's hair. If my clients have been poorly, I go round to their homes.

I think our rates are very cheap compared to the mainland. I charge £3.95 for a shampoo and set, a blow dry is £4.50, basic trim £3.70 and £5.50 for a complete re-style. Visitors come and say, 'Gosh, isn't that cheap,' but the locals don't think so. We have to pay very high rates because of the price of property here. It's the same as the middle of London, but it's unfair because our wages are very low.

People on the off-islands have their weekly shopping days to St Mary's and they fit an appointment in then. Visitors feel coming here by boat is part of island life but if they don't want to come, they live like the locals and have the windswept look.

Marcia Sandford, forty-two, comes from a family with a long history on Scilly. She went to college in Cornwall for a City and Guilds' course in hairdressing, returned to Scilly and set up her own salon, Seawaves. She is divorced with two sons.

I keep open in the winter and more visitors seem to be coming. I don't know why because it's cold and wet and windy. I think they come for the peace. I said to a lady last year, 'Whatever are you doing here this time of the year?' And she said, 'Well, I can throw my bike in the door, leave the door open, go for a walk, say cheerio to the kids and tell them to go to the beach and play, and I can relax. You can't do that abroad.'

We don't finish in the summer until 6.30 or 7 p.m., but after that I'm out of my salon and into my little boat. I spend as much time on the water as I can – a boat on Scilly is as important as a car. You've only got a few miles of road so you can't just jump in a car and go somewhere.

THE HOSPITAL COOK

I came back to Scilly two years ago to be the cook at St Mary's Hospital. It's a little cottage hospital with fourteen beds, you know most of the people who come in, and I'm able to chat with them about their diets. I cook for any

Jo Gooding, thirty-one, comes from Wales and moved here with her family about eighteen years ago. She worked in the dairy and in a hotel, went to Australia for six months, lived in Wales for a couple of years and, in 1989, sailed for nine months as a cook on *The Maiden* in Whitbread's Round the World race.

number from between two and fourteen patients. They get spoilt rotten.

It's like cooking for your family. They are mainly old folks who just like meat and two veg. You get your regulars in, those with diabetes, for instance. If they're having a problem getting their sugar level right, they come in and it's sorted out. I'm on five day, split shifts, 8 a.m. to 2 p.m. and 5 to 7 p.m. I cook for the staff too.

It's such an easy life here. I walk up to work in the morning, you see someone coming over in their boat, it's just so nice. But I want to work with children with special needs – I'd like to teach them sailing – so I may move back to the mainland.

THE WHOLESALERS AND . . .

Gerry: The company is unique because it's a wholesalers-cum-cash-and-carry-cum-retail. You couldn't have that on the mainland, but you have to do it here because of the limited space and number of people. We've avoided treading on people's toes – there are other things we could sell but don't because the balance of the island trade needs to be kept. We've had too many shops turned into cafés which shouldn't have been. For businesses here to survive, I think they need to recognize the tourist, but be capable of servicing the local community as well. You *can* run a gift shop and just be open in the summer, but if everyone did that, you'd end up with a dormitory in the winter.

It is very expensive, freightwise, to get goods here and the big advantage of a company like ours is that, if we buy sufficiently large cases from major manufacturers, they deliver what they call 'carriage paid home' with the freight charge paid by them. So we can now sell goods at the same price as they are on the mainland.

Why become a councillor? Probably the difference between someone like me who came to live here and the Scillonian who lives here all the time, is that I've got quite

Gerry, fifty-three, and Pat Twynham, fifty-two, come from Northamptonshire. Gerry joined the Army as a boy entrant, worked in a factory as a technical engineer and foreman, and opened a small garage. Pat worked in the Income Tax Office before having children. In 1985 they came to live in Scilly and now run Isles of Scilly Wholesale Provisions Ltd, and Trevean Guest House. Gerry was elected a councillor in 1993.

a good knowledge of the mainland as well, specially of industry, and I think the Council could probably be run better if it had more businessmen on it. But it is a good example of how the Government would like all councils to be, because it runs the islands completely. I'd like to try and make it cheaper for people to travel here, but any changes have got to be what local people want – I came here to live because the islands are what they are, not to change them.

... THE BED & BREAKFAST PEOPLE

Pat: I think people like coming to a B&B because they enjoy eating out and there are lots of places doing evening meals with prices to suit everyone. With what we charge (£14 a night) they don't expect all the frills, but they do get a good comfortable bed and a full breakfast: bacon, sausages, eggs, potatoes, waffles, fritters, beans, tomatoes, mushrooms. We don't have a menu, but if anyone says they'd like something else, we'll give it to them because we're cheap and cheerful. You go to a hotel and don't always get that much choice. And the rooms are spotlessly clean, thanks to my daughter, Sally, who does them for me. When she was little, I always used to say my dream was to have somebody do my housework, and she said to me the other day, 'Mum, you didn't realize it would be me who would be your char, did you?'

Lots of people come back. I think they must just like the atmosphere – we've got a family coming next week for their fourth time. We try to make it a home from home for visitors – let them come and go as they please. They don't want somebody standing on the doorstep saying don't do this, don't do that, wipe your feet before you come in.

THE VET

Dr Malcolm Martland, forty-one, was born in Liverpool, graduated in veterinary medicine at Cambridge, practised in Oxford for two years, worked for the Ministry of Agriculture, Ross Poultry, and the Agricultural Research Council. In 1986 he was employed as a veterinary pathologist with the Swiss company Sandoz and took a Doctorate at Berne University before returning to Britain to set up a veterinary consultancy. He came to Scilly in November 1992.

I was warned there would not be enough work to make a living here as a vet, so I combine it with my consultancy work. I also do quite a lot of routine operations which the previous vet didn't do. My main interest is veterinary pathology.

Yes, I do feel cut off and isolated. That's one reason I like it here! It's lovely on a day like today, the fog's closing in, no planes, nothing. If it wasn't for the ship, there'd be no post – that would be very good too. There aren't any real problems except the agricultural livestock – that's an economic one – the numbers have declined so much over the years there's not enough farming going on. The main work I do for farmers is artificial insemination of cattle, which is not really a veterinary job but it helps them economically and helps me too. I do a lot of Ministry of Agriculture testing for tuberculosis and brucellosis, but most of the things I see are routine rather than fire brigade work.

We had a spate of cattle swallowing potatoes – if they're not chopped or chewed enough, they get stuck in their throat and the cow starts to blow up because it can't belch properly. There are several ways of curing this. One is to stick a spike in the side of the animal and pull the plunger out to release the gas; the other is to put a stomach tube down, and this is much less drastic. But, of course, all the farmers having seen the stomach tube technique now have got bits of gas pipe, and do it themselves! It's very simple, it just lets the gas out and pushes the potato out of the way.

There's not a large population of dogs. I maybe see four or five a day. It's routine stuff – bites, scratches, annual vaccinations, and everyone seems to be mad keen on worming their animals. Off-islanders tend to ring up and ask if I can meet them at the quay because they have boat schedules to stick to, unless they come in their own boat. We quite often have a consultation in the waiting-room there for rabbits, the school pet rat (it had a cold recently), cats and dogs.

I think islanders had all their own conservation measures in place long before bureaucrats started meddling with it and there does seem to be a conflict of interest between what bureaucrats think is environmental protection and what is agriculture. In fact, agriculture can be the very thing we need for environmental protection but we only hear bad things about it, like nitrates in the water. You don't hear that grazing encourages certain kinds of wild flowers to grow and if you leave the ground to go back to nature, it gets covered in bracken and gorse and all the wild flowers die. People have cared for the land for thousands of years and I don't see why they shouldn't carry on, provided they don't step out of line and spray the place with dialdrin or dioxin. Otherwise it just turns the islands into a non-productive tourist attraction.

I was told they used to have Auks because islanders controlled the Black-backed Gulls, culling them almost naturally by hat-pinning the eggs before they hatched. There's little snippets like this that you hear from the past which just stick. We imagine progress is good for us, but it isn't necessarily. People can destroy the ground they set out to protect.

THE HOTEL MANAGERS

Richard, forty-one, and Fiona Chantrey, thirty-four, have been general managers of Tregarthen's Hotel, one of the Best Western group, for the last ten years. Both worked for Trust House Forte before coming to Scilly. They have a young son.

Richard: The hotel started in 1848 in a little cottage where a Captain Tregarthen lived with his family and owned a steamship which was the Royal Mail packet for the islands. He brought the boat to and from Penzance once or twice a week with the first tourists to the island, to stay in his cottage. The ghost here is said to be his daughter Mary, who hanged herself in one of the rooms, which is now sealed off. Harry, our gardener who's been with the hotel for about thirty-five years, reckons he met Mary one day in the corridor and says she was a very friendly ghost. They had quite a chat. Apparently, she was telling him all about the past, and he was telling her how hard he had to work, fetching coal up to the bedrooms, they all had fireplaces then.

Weather is our main problem. When the fog comes down, the planes don't fly, we can't get guests out or in, freight supplies can get stuck, lost, delivered to different hotels. But we don't have crime, fights or vandalism. We went away last winter for three weeks, and I said to Fiona on the way to the airport, 'Did you lock the house?' Well, neither did I. And it sat unlocked for three weeks and no one went anywhere near it.

It's difficult to have a private life here. I can't take Fiona out to dinner and have a nice quiet meal on our own. We go out, but know everyone in the restaurant. A few years ago I did get very claustrophobic – I felt the grass was greener on the other side, but didn't want to leave, the quality of life here is excellent. So I learnt to fly and bought myself a little four-seater Cessna plane, and I can now zoom off to the mainland at my will. Sometimes I pop over just for a cup of coffee, then come back fighting fit. And maybe on a Sunday, when there's no transport to the islands and there's an emergency, the island people know the plane's there and I'll fly it for them. It's all unofficial. I don't charge them for it. But they have to put up with the noise of the plane going on and off the island, and if I can repay them like this, I will.

Fiona: As my family are from the Isle of Arran in Scotland, I felt quite okay about coming to Scilly. But you have to be a lot more organized working on an island and have contingency plans, for instance, if the boat is delayed. Of course, if people can't leave because of fog, others can't arrive and it tends to work itself out. But if guests are leaving by helicopter and that doesn't fly, and your arrivals are coming by boat which does come in, you do have a problem. You ask them how important it is that they reach the mainland that day and if it's crucial, we advise them to take the boat because they'll definitely get there. People say, 'What do you think it's going to do? Is it going to clear up?' And I say if I knew the answer to that, I'd make a lot more money than I do being a hotel manager. You have to be slightly vague without sounding as if it's not our problem. It is our problem. Our responsibility ends when they leave the island, not when they leave the front door of our hotel.

I do sometimes miss being anonymous. Not often, because it is nice to say 'hello' to everyone when you walk down the street. And deep down, when visitors are around, you sort of click with other islanders and there's a feeling of support from everyone. Before I came I was told, 'What you think in the morning, somebody will let you know by lunch-time.' And it's quite true.

THE CUSTOMS OFFICER

Len Smith, forty-nine, was born in Liverpool and came to Scilly three years ago. He has been in the Customs and Excise Department for thirty years, and is married with two children.

There's no such thing as a typical day. Yacht traffic is very unpredictable – they appear from the mainland, Europe, the Caribbean or even straight from the USA – you never know what you might meet when you go out on patrol.

My overall role is basically enforcing the law as regards the import of prohibited and restricted goods and items such as drugs, firearms, animals and pornography. These are the things we're looking for. We have a 28 ft launch and patrol the islands every day subject to weather conditions, of course. We try to talk to as many yacht people as possible, as we're increasingly reliant on their help in combatting the drugs and arms traffickers.

Island people here are very law abiding, they're very mindful of what goes on out there on the water because they're interested in ships. I believe that most people would tell me or my colleagues if they saw something funny going on. Visiting Customs teams come from the mainland to help cover the yacht traffic, I have a colleague for the summer months and someone's always on the end of a phone. I also co-operate with the local police and can get help very quickly when I want it.

As well as being the Customs Officer, I'm the Immigration Officer, and collect Light Dues for Trinity House. I've also been the Receiver of Wreck which involves, among other things, removing teeth and skin samples from stranded dolphins and porpoises for the Natural History Museum.

I'm on a five year posting here of which I've done three. I've enjoyed it and my wife has too. My children have probably had the best education they would get anywhere.

Jacky Pritchard, fifty-one, was born in Cardiff. A former classical ballet dancer, she also swam for the Welsh Squad, became Welsh diving champion at eighteen, Welsh trampolene champion, and British trampolene champion at twenty. Now she trains children for The Entertainers, runs the Harbourside Hotel on the quay with her husband, Tony, and they have six children.

THE CHILDREN'S PRODUCER

At present we have eight nine- to fourteen-year-olds in The Entertainers. It's a good number – if you have more it gets a bit like a bun fight in the dressing-room. There are only two boys. You don't go out and ask boys, you have to wait for them to come. I think they get a bit teased. But there's a local dancing school and they come from there.

We start rehearsing in September, with a three week break in October/November when many people involved in tourism have a holiday. On the first Saturday in February, we provide a free tea and entertainment for all the senior citizens in the Town Hall. We have a different theme each year – this time we're doing the Common Market countries. Next year is our fortieth anniversary and we'll probably do something special.

You don't get older teenagers in the show because by the time they're fourteen or fifteen they're getting too self-conscious and don't want to do it. They've got to take their GCSEs at sixteen, then 99 per cent of them go away. The age gap in the show is very big – the next group is in the thirties, our oldest is sixty-seven. You can't have a young romantic lead; you just have to make it funny.

Our audiences are mainly middle-aged people. I think the show is taking them back to their grass roots, their life before television. It's live entertainment and very cheap – £2 a ticket, I think. But it's local people and the policeman's in it, and they'll see him on the street the next day. Visitors write to Betty Sylvester, the secretary, to find out when the show and the play are on so they can work their holiday around it. They're on alternate weeks, Wednesday and Thursday nights. We always say there's no smut, this is a family show where you can take your great-grandma down to your grandchild and they all enjoy it.

THE TWENTY-ONE-YEAR-OLD

When I went to school on the mainland at sixteen, I already knew lots of people in Truro, though I did get homesick. But I think you have to go away at that age – it's when you really start to grow up and it was the best thing I could ever have done. If I'd gone into digs and had to fend for myself, I'm not quite sure I would have managed. But in the

Emma Pritchard, twenty-one, is one of Jacky and Tony Pritchard's six children. Since leaving school she has worked in a kitchen in Italy and now plans to study hotel management.

school, you're under their control and they help you through any problems. But you're still able to do your own thing and you do gain independence.

It is a very sheltered life here and it was eye-opening to go to the mainland and see how the other half live. There were so many people. And so many facilities available to you that you don't have in Scilly. There's not much sport here, though you have running and horse riding, but over there you have absolutely everything.

But although you miss out on things here like the cinema and bowling alleys, there are other advantages, like going out in boats, which other children will never have had. If I was bringing up children, I'd like to do it over here. You can trust them to go out and know they'll come back.

THE ACCOMPANIST

John Crane, sixty-nine, worked for the Credential Insurance Company, and came to Scilly with his wife when he retired. He plays the piano for The Entertainers, Melody Time, and the Choral Society. They have four children.

There was a time when both the Choral Society and The Entertainers were finding it extremely difficult to find a pianist and when we came down on holiday, they asked me to play for them. I said I'd be pleased to, so when we arrived the first thing I had to do was start practising and rehearsing. I tried to fit in two or three concerts while we were here, but The Entertainers was a bit different – you needed to rehearse it thoroughly. So they asked me if I could put all the music for next year's show on tape.

I've always regarded myself as an accompanist and I try to follow my soloists, not dictate to them. So to put something on tape without them was a bit tricky. However, I did it, and when we came on holiday the following year, we went to the show and saw the result and I must admit I was amazed how they coped. I was listening to my own tape and they were singing to it!

When you have a full-time job, you say, 'Won't it be lovely when we retire, if the weather looks good, we can go off somewhere for a week.' Not so with us, because throughout the summer, the Choral Society is most Mondays, The

Entertainers on Wednesdays and Thursdays every other week, and the play (my wife has produced this for a couple of years) the other weeks. We do want to go away in the summer next year, but feel almost guilty about it.

THE BALLROOM DANCER

When I was about eight years old, my cousin got married and they were dancing at the reception. I told Mum that I'd love to start dancing and she said, 'Well, we'll have a look around.' So I started. As a child I got my Bronze, Silver and Gold and the six bars in ballroom dancing and Latin American. At fourteen, I began going in for competition work, and helping young children with the Beginners Waltz and the Quick Step.

Nineteen months ago, we started ballroom dancing in the church hall, and we've recently become a club. We now have about twenty-eight members and as many as fifty people come during the holiday season. Visitors are always relaxed and can make it a very nice evening and if anyone gets stuck on a step they can't do, we can give them individual teaching. We do the waltz, quickstep, foxtrot, tango, cha-cha-cha, jiving, St Bernard's Waltz, military two-step, barn dances. Fortunately Janet Baker, a former dancing teacher now in her eighties, kept all her records and has lent them to the club.

Lynne Marshall, forty-one, came to live on Scilly when her mother bought a hairdresser's salon here. After marrying, she left to live on the mainland, but returned four years ago. She has been a hairdresser, and in self-catering for thirteen years. She is now divorced and has two sons.

We have an age range from twenty-one to sixty-five and people who come include teachers and councillors and even one or two of the young boatmen who thoroughly enjoy it. I think they suddenly decided they wanted to learn to dance properly – men always think it's a cissy thing to do. One day I'd like to start a school – that's one of my dreams.

I think the islands should have ballroom dancing. There are a lot of tea dances on the mainland now and it's becoming fashionable. We're a holiday place, so we might as well be with it.

THE MUSEUM SECRETARY

Steve Ottery, sixty-three, born in Nottingham and a former teacher, came to Scilly in 1966 when the new comprehensive school opened. He served in the Navy, was a youth employment officer, ran the boarding hostel on Scilly when it started, and has taken walking tours round the island with his wife, Julia.

The museum came about because of the discovery in 1963 of the *Nor Nour* treasures. There had been a small museum here before, but over the years most of the precious items found on the island had gone to the British Museum, Penwith or Plymouth. It was put about that if a proper museum could be found, these would be allowed to stay on the island. So two ladies, Murley MacLaran, the wife of the late Land Steward, and her friend Mary Mackenzie, started one. There were public subscriptions, exhibitions of what had been found, and a businessman put up £15,000 with no interest, which we had to pay back over the years. The building was built in 1967 and we now get about £10,000 revenue plus some grants, and entrance money goes to the general upkeep. We're a little bit in hand, but rates, rents and insurance come to £1,500. We're open from Easter until the end of October and after that it's Wednesday afternoons only or by appointment. On a good year we get twenty thousand visitors.

There are fourteen committee members and nobody is paid except two part-time cleaners. We occasionally buy items, but things are nearly always given or loaned. Everything has to be made on Scilly, used here or wrecked here and if we don't know what something is, we call on the Cornwall Archaeological and Biological Units.

I'm always amazed how much is taken away from Scilly. I don't really mind – if every unusual pebble or flint was brought in, we shouldn't have anywhere to put them. Quite often we say to people who bring things for us to see, 'If you get tired of it, please send it back, or remember us in your will', and it's amazing how many people do. I think if I had to choose one single favourite piece, it would be the gold posy ring found in the treasures on the wreck of *The Association*. Or Sir Cloudesley Shovell's chamber-pot, which was christened by the diver who brought it to the surface after it had been on the sea-bed for 267 years!

THE TOUR DRIVERS

Bruce Maple: The visitors loved Ron's sense of humour because it was so dry. The things he'd say on his tour, I could never say. You just couldn't copy his style, it would be an insult to his memory. It was very simple and to the point, he wasn't one for being flowery but the thing that was his hallmark was that he always looked so miserable. We once had a coach party of deaf and dumb people and they were sat in the Comer Avenger that he used to drive. I was explaining to those at the back what Father (in law) was saying, and they were very amused because his expression throughout the tour never changed. He never laughed. And this is what the visitors loved about him.

Uncle Vic was something else and the tours are named after him. He used to do the airport run and when he retired in 1970, some visitors said to him, 'Why don't you do island tours, and call them Vic's Tours?' and that was how they started. When Vic did them, they used to take two or three hours, it was a concert on wheels basically. He'd stop and talk to the cows. I'm not quite sure what he said, Uncle Vic had a language of his own. But he could recite poetry and sing and was an entertainer for seventy-odd years. In fact, he was one of the founder members of the Scillonian Entertainers.

Fred Elms: There are four of us doing the bus tour now, but as there are only 7 miles of road, there aren't many different places you can go. Mine doesn't start until 11 a.m., so I have another little job as well, cleaning one of the pubs every morning. I try and keep the commentary light-hearted, there are enough true stories without making them up. A couple of years ago, a very rare bird arrived from North America called the Grey-cheeked Thrush. It landed on the Garrison and it was only the second time anyone had ever seen one in England. Three hundred bird-watchers rushed to the spot and were looking through their binoculars when, all of a sudden out of the hedgerow, a great big ginger tom-cat arrived and ate the bird and there was nothing they could do about it.

Bruce Maple was born on the Devon/Cornwall border. He was a restaurant manager in Oxford, came to Scilly for a summer in 1976, married Veronica and started helping her father, Ron Perry, with his round-the-island coach trips. He now takes the tours himself. Here, he remembers the late Ron Perry and Ron's uncle, Vic Trenwith, who started the tours.

Fred Elms, forty-seven, from Enfield in north London, came to live in Scilly in 1977 after spending holidays here for fourteen years. Two years ago he started doing tours round St Mary's in a sixteen-seater mini bus.

THE GARDENER

June Lethbridge, sixty-two, was born a few yards from where she now lives and worked on her father's farm. She is Sunday school superintendent in the Methodist chapel, an artist, singer and one of the producers of The Entertainers. She is married to Richard, also a singer, and they have two children and two grandchildren.

We've always been keen on gardening and always fancied a sub-tropical one for St Mary's as well as Tresco. We thought these 2 acres of land owned by the Duchy would make a good one and now rent them for the people of St Mary's – it was £25 a year to start with, but is now £40 and we've no way of making any money for it. In the beginning, we sent a circular to every house and I got about thirty replies. A lot of people gave us money and said they'd help with the landscaping – it was a former quarry, all rough ground and brambles.

We managed to get enough help to tame it to a certain extent and now an elderly couple look after two beds. We've had memorial seats donated, and some which the Council didn't want any more; the Council digger has moved some earth, the Duchy have been in with their tractors for the long grass, but there's nobody to keep it looking like it should.

Quite a lot of visitors come here – it says Rest Area outside – and more offer to work than locals. They'll pick a corner and clean it. I used to leave a pan with a trowel, and every time I came down it was full of weeds. Last year I advertised for helpers, and one day we had six visitors working, but not one local. They say the garden's lovely, but that's as far as it goes. I'm going to have another go trying to get children on it. The Girl Guides came down once and did a good job, and I thought, 'Oh, lovely, they'll be doing this every year', but they didn't. The Environmental Trust Support Group did some work one day, and booked two more dates, but the Secretary forgot to put the notice up, so no one came.

My husband cuts the grass and I work at it too, but I want an army to come and help. If it was suddenly cleaned one day, you don't know what you'd find underneath.

THE BAKERS

Terry Parsons, fifty-seven, was a National Westminster Bank manager before taking over the Kavorna Bakery and Gift Shop six years ago with his wife, Elizabeth, a former nursing auxiliary. They have three grown-up children.

We always thought it would be wonderful to retire here in due course and then we saw this place was on the market. We tossed a coin a few times, scratched our heads and thought shall we or shan't we, and eventually decided to have a go. Elizabeth ran it alone until I was able to give up my job.

I could barely boil an egg when I first started but we managed to keep one of the existing staff, and were flying by the seat of our pants for a while. Now we have a very skilled baker working with us and from the basic three varieties of bread we did at the beginning, we have granary, white, wholemeal, mixed grain, rye, cheese and onion, French bread, and bloomers with sesame seed on top. We make over sixty varieties of cakes, Cornish pasties and a cheese one which, apart from the lard, is a good alternative for vegetarians. In high summer we make up to 800 loaves a day, 700 to 800 rolls and 4,000 little cakes a week.

We supply the off-islands as well, so we have to make sure the production run is ready for the boat. It depends on the tide – if it's midday, it's easy, but if you have a 7 a.m. boat to catch, you have to alter the baking schedule to make sure everything is baked and cool ready to pack away in boxes to ship across.

Elizabeth delivers to anyone who wants it, and we don't charge for this. She gets up about 6 a.m., stocks the shop up, packs the bread for the off-islands, and makes the sandwiches. I've no regrets about making the swap from banking to baking and the thing we miss with pleasure are those wretched four wheels and driving up and down the motorway.

THE BULB SELLER

Peter Guy, fifty, who owns The Bulb Shop in Hugh Town, can trace his family on his mother's side to the mid-1300s, and on his father's side, from Port Isaac in Cornwall, to about 1654. His wife died in 1992.

The Scilly bulbs are daffodils, narcissi and iris and next to tourism, the island's bulbs are its main industry. I sell a few tons a year but I also import some from Holland. I'm afraid so. But it's those I can't get here anyway: tulips, crocus, hyacinths and lilliums. The magenta gladioli – they call them Whistling Jacks – are flowering now and we get the bulbs in the middle of June.

What's so special about Scilly bulbs? Nothing really! If you bought King Arthur off me this summer and planted them in your garden where you already had King Arthur from the mainland, ours would flower earlier the first year, but then they'd gradually revert to the slightly later time after that. We're approximately a month earlier than the mainland, even Cornwall.

THE MASSEUSE

I was the first business like this to start on Scilly, and when we opened, people didn't understand about massage and made jokes about it. Now I've got a twelve-seater sauna, solarium and two showers and I do facials and massage. A full body massage is £15, £7.50 for a part-massage. And everyone says, 'What parts?'

At first I thought, because everyone knows me, the locals would be a bit apprehensive and I never talk about who has come. The best advertisement is when they go out and say it was great. Doctors now send people to me and I go to Park House, too, the old folks' home, to do their hands and feet and knees. I make some of my own oils and ointments, particularly from marigolds and grow my own comfrey – that's wonderful for knitting bones.

We get a lot of yacht people using the showers, and stewards off the *Scillonian* ring up in the morning as soon as the ship arrives, to have a sauna with a massage afterwards. Ladies who tie flowers here get bad backs, and several farmers' wives say to their husbands, 'Why don't you go and see if Dot can sort you out.' I think farmers are quite shocked to think they have come to such a thing as a massage, but when they go out they say, 'Oh, I must come here again.'

Dot Elvin, sixty-one, was born in Castle Bromwich. Her parents moved to Scilly, but she nursed on the mainland until thirty-six years ago, when she returned to live here. She continued nursing, qualified as a masseuse, and is a member of the Association of Natural Medicine. Three years ago she opened the Venture Leisure Club and a video shop on the industrial estate. She has one son.

THE BOUTIQUE OWNER

I never thought of myself as a shopkeeper and still don't – when the sky's blue, I can be out on my boat in five minutes. I opened this shop to sell leather work for a friend. But within three or four years we'd bought next door, and next door again. It just snowballed up the street. Our strength is Jane's buying – she injects all the fashion into it and we're an open all the year round, locally-run, locally-owned shop.

We have three shops now and I don't think it would be socially acceptable to expand. I've had opportunities to do other things but I don't want to spread all over the island like a rash. I'm doing well, and I don't need any more. It's a good living, but I really think it's our relationship with people that matters – that's what it's down to.

I do feel that the service industries in Scilly need to analyse their performance. There is a bit of a take it or leave it attitude now and I think we have a collective responsibility to ensure people enjoy coming to Scilly and are given a good service, though it's a delicate balance between being like the mainland and retaining our differentness. We could do more for visiting yachtsmen and I've been in a restaurant where six people arrived at 8.30 p.m.

Terry Ward, thirty-seven, was born on the island of an old Scillonian family, worked in shops on the mainland and as a children's play leader with Lambeth Borough Council. Now he runs The Foredeck and Foredeck Too boutiques with his wife, Jane, is a governor of the primary school, on the board of the Steamship Company, sings in the choir, and plays the harmonica in a local band. They have two daughters.

to be turned away because the chef was just washing the dishes. I just get the feeling over the last few years that we are slightly complacent. Everything that is beautiful about Scilly is God-given; architecturally, though, it's boring. So I think we should do that little bit more on the human side because the environment we live in deserves it.

I was talking to one of the boatmen the other day, who said that visitors who've been here for three or four or sometimes ten years tend to see more of the negative side, but a first-timer sees it differently. He told me how he took a first-time visitor out on his boat to the Eastern Isles, landed on St Agnes, had lunch in the pub there, and on the way back in the boat, this guy told him it was the best day he'd ever had in his life. He'd just seen the good things. Possibly the longer people stay here, the more they start moaning about cars, dogs and prices. Perhaps I'm turning into a whinge bucket! But it would be hard to find somewhere to knock spots off Scilly. I've never seen better beaches anywhere.

THE GARDEN RESTAURANT OWNER

We thought very carefully about the name – we wanted to tell people it was out of doors, to dress sensibly and to expect what they were going to get. Now, even after twelve years, it's still a great pleasure for me to serve food that people say, 'Oh, isn't that lovely.' I make scones every afternoon – probably about ten thousand over a summer season – and I love making spicy apple pies. There's something terribly homely about them. I also make an old-fashioned seedy cake which the older customers love, and things like crab cocktail with cucumber mayonnaise, red onion tart, a vegetable terrine with a red pepper sauce, and Mrs Osborne's Savoury Brazil Nut Slice. I try new things all the time and use local suppliers if possible. Kavorna Bakery do a special loaf for me and I've made them promise they won't make it for anyone else. It's a big round one that they divide lightly into four and I slit the sections twice and fill them with chicken and salad, patés and crab and beef.

Our sons have all been born with us both working, but we're always very careful to have Sundays together as a family. We go camping on St Martin's for a weekend in June which is great fun. I just cook ahead for the restaurant and make sure everything is taken care of. I have a mother's help who helps with the change-overs in our two holiday homes as well as with the children. I like to give lots of dinner parties too, because if you don't, you end up doing nothing but work.

Women do work tremendously hard over here, very few are housewives. One of the reasons I wanted to have 'Juliet's Garden' was because I didn't want to be one of the girls who married one of the local May boys. Andrew was delighted after a couple of years when he was in a pub one day and heard someone say, 'Who's that?' referring to him, and the answer was, 'Juliet's husband'.

Juliet May, forty-three, went to Eastbourne School of Domestic Economy and worked in advertising in London. She is married to Andrew, who took over the running of Seaways Flower Farm when his father retired, and she opened Juliet's Garden Restaurant in 1981. They have three children.

THE GIFT SHOP OWNERS

Ian's idea was to set up a business to cater for something on the island that wasn't being catered for in a big way, and that was island crafts. We have a lot of gifted people here who need an outlet for their work – there's the monthly craft market in the Town Hall, but they do need a steady income.

Now we sell soft toys, wooden objects, pottery, tatting, lace, home-made marmalade, lampshade stands and weed pots made from wreck wood, puppets and mobiles, plants and seeds. We also have a gallery at Porth Loo because there isn't enough space here for pictures and prints. We've built up our stock from what people tell us: islanders have come in and said there's nothing to do in the winter evenings. Nobody stocks embroidery kits and they had to wait until they went to the mainland or do mail order. So we brought these in and they're very popular.

Rose Tabraham, fifty-six, a former primary school teacher from Bristol who took early retirement, runs the Turnstone Gift Shop in Hugh Town with her husband, Ian, whom she met on the islands.

Shopkeepers try to sell different things and not step on each other's toes because we all have to survive. A lot don't stay open in winter because they want to keep below the VAT threshold – if you go over it, it costs a lot more and you might as well stay open and try and get some money back.

These islands have a magic about them which is most strange. If you're right for the islands things seem to fall into place. Those who don't really fit in, don't stay.

THE AIRPORT MANAGER

My job description is to keep the airport running for the operators, so if you look out of the window at the runway, the lighting, the fire-engine, it's down to me to make sure they are all running well.

On an average day there are about eight helicopter flights and twenty Skybus planes. On a Saturday there are around forty flights, though it's quieter in the winter. We also get private planes coming for the day. There are no night flights, there's no demand, but we'd open the airport if there was an emergency. We've recently been given the

Customs' concession whereby we can accept some Continental aircraft direct, without them having to go to the mainland first.

In October the Council took the airport under their wing. I'd say most of the changes they've made were needed, though there are one or two which people have a knock at, and one is the luggage conveyers. People used to get off the plane and walk to where the buses are; the luggage trolleys came down, people took their luggage off them, and got straight into the bus. It took about seven or eight minutes, and in the winter everyone moaned about waiting in the cold. Now people walk through an automatic door and wait inside, the luggage is put on an automatic belt which takes it inside, and people take it off that. But, of course, this isn't Scilly. This is always the enigma of the islands: the attraction is to stay a little bit, not behind the times, but behind the mainland. On the other hand, people who come here want modern services. So there's always this battle.

Neil Hayley, forty-nine, was a PE teacher for thirteen years and played cricket for Cornwall. In 1980 he came to Tresco to look after the Abbey, and his wife, Mary, to do the cooking for the Dorrien Smith family. He was involved in setting up the first runway for British Airways Helicopters to fly into Tresco, became heliport manager when the operation started in 1983, and in January 1993 airport manager at St Mary's. He has three grown-up children.

THE RESTAURANT/DISCO OWNER AND CHEF

I do the cooking for the restaurant with my wife and son, and we're open seven days a week for breakfasts, lunches, and evening meals. The disco is the only place staff from other restaurants, pubs and hotels can come to after they finish work at 11 p.m. – it's all underground, so there's no noise whatsoever. I'm there every night behind the bar and really enjoy it. We get about a hundred and fifty people on Fridays and Saturdays and about seventy to a hundred the other nights. It costs £2 to come in, but it depends on the time of year. A lot of students haven't got any money at all, so you let them in cheaper.

October is our busiest time. It's when the twitchers (bird-watchers) come and they hold their log meetings downstairs. They're so keen and dedicated and there are

Barry Wright, forty-four, was born on Scilly. He has worked in Torquay and St Mary's and is now managing director of The Porthcressa Restaurant, which incorporates a fish and chip shop and a disco, the only one on the island. He is married to Sue, who has the catering concession at St Mary's airport. They have two sons, Mark, the disco DJ, and Conrad, who helps in the kitchen.

lots of families and young people. We have a little CB on the roof so they can get in touch with bird-watchers on Tresco and someone always mans it during the day, sitting there with a pad. A voice will crackle through saying there's something to be seen on Bryher, and they all run off and hire a boat and get over there.

THE COLLECTOR

Nick Millard, forty-five, was born and brought up in Walsall in the West Midlands. He went to horticultural college in Wolverhampton and when his parents retired to Scilly seventeen years ago, he came with them. He has a large collection of scavenged treasures and has raised £15,000 for charities in the last five years.

It was a bit difficult at first, asking people for money, but after a while you get into it and it's a regular thing with me now, doing a couple of hours every night. I raised £6,262 for cancer research last year and this year, in three months, I've raised £1,579 for the British Heart Foundation. It's a different charity each year, but it has to be a good one because I put a lot of work into it. This afternoon, I'll be going up to the airport and every night I go to all the pubs and hotels, never miss.

When I'm not collecting money, I like hunting for things on the beach. These are all my bead necklaces – it takes me about a month to make one. Some of the beads are very old, some moderately so. These tiny bottles were for perfume and these for poison. Some have 'Not to be Taken' on them, and others have lines going across for blind people to know they're poison.

This is a piece of coal from the *Italia* sunk in 1917 off St Agnes. A diver got that for me from the wreck. All these little bodies and legs of dolls are of porcelain, German pottery, mid-nineteenth century. These old clay pipes are from 1680 to 1880 and this old brandy bottle is dated 1804.

What I like to see, and I normally get shot when I say this, is a north-westerly hurricane that's coming into the harbour on a big tide and smashes all the beach up. You go down after the storm, and you can't go wrong. But you say that to someone who's got a boat there, and I'm not very popular.

THE FISHMONGER

I know it seems funny, but some of the restaurants and hotels get fish from the mainland though most are happy to phone me and ask what I've got that day and take what's caught. Most of the time, especially in the height of the season, we have a job to catch enough to keep everyone I supply happy. Fridays are still the traditional fish day in the guest-houses, though not the hotels, who have it every day.

In the winter months I used to do up old buildings and I worked for the previous owner on what is now my restaurant. I liked the way it turned out and said to him, jokingly, that if he ever thought of selling I'd buy the premises. Two years later he sold it to me. I now have a chef and the restaurant is open every day except Sunday.

Peter Thompson, forty-eight, a Scillonian, worked on passenger boats for holiday divers and now runs the fish shop and the Galley Fish Restaurant with the fish supplied by his brother, David.

TRESCO

Tresco, north of St Mary's and the second largest island, is wild and rugged in the north, has sub-tropical gardens and white sandy beaches in the south, and green fields and farmland in the centre. A priory was founded here by Benedictine monks in the twelfth century, but only crumbling walls remain today. The famous Abbey Gardens were started by Augustus Smith, Lord Proprietor of Scilly from 1834 to 1872, who not only planned the gardens, but introduced compulsory education on the islands thirty years before it became law in the UK.

The island is a private estate leased by the Duchy of Cornwall to the Dorrien Smith family who live in the Abbey House. A landing fee is charged for visitors arriving by boat; helicopter passengers arrive at the world's only garden heliport, which opened in 1983. There are no private cars allowed but The Island Hotel provides a buggy service for visitors. There is a school, a church, a shop, the centuries old New Inn, holiday and time-share cottages.

The 17 acre garden has plants which grow nowhere else in Britain, many from seedlings brought back by ships' captains in the last century. A Yucca Whipper which flowers only once in twenty years, grew 12 ft in fourteen days in 1991 and gained an entry in the *Guinness Book of Records*. In the unusually harsh winters of 1987 and 1990, hundreds of plants and trees were lost, but with the help of botanical gardens around the world, it is hard now to see where the damage occurred. Adjoining the gardens is the Valhalla collection of shipheads. King Charles Castle was built in 1550, Cromwell's Castle, a 60 ft high round tower to strengthen the islands against invasion by the Dutch, a century later.

THE ISLAND PROPRIETOR

My family got virtually wiped out in the Second World War – my father lost three brothers, an uncle and two first cousins. He had an estate in Somerset but returned to run Tresco in the early '50s when my grandfather was ill. He started the island going in the direction it is now, because he realized that flower farming was never going to support the community.

My original ancestors had enormous fortunes, and although their land holdings weren't necessarily profitable, the Big House supported the whole community. This was fine, provided the one in the middle could afford it. But when wages started increasing and you had to pay heavy taxes through the 1960s and 1970s, this kind of estate couldn't survive unless there was a business to bring in money from outside. It was always drummed into me by every advisor I've ever had, that the place has to pay for itself. And in order to justify employing a large number of people, you have to have a business capable of doing so.

Flower growing was the main industry here and very profitable between 1880 and 1950. But then the jet plane brought in flowers from all over the world and changed the face of the market. People no longer had to buy narcissi in January or February, because that was all that was available. There were forty-five men on the farm here in 1950, now we have two permanent employees though I think we're still the biggest farm in the islands.

If I'd inherited the island now, knowing what I do about running a business or life in general, I'd find it daunting, but then, well, it was there and I'd got to do it. Tresco was an agricultural estate then. It's now a leisure estate. We're providing services of all sorts to a community of holiday-makers and it's this that keeps our community alive. It pays the wages, pays for maintenance of the houses, the roads,

Robert Dorrien Smith, forty-two, read English at Oxford and went to agricultural college in Cirencester. When his father died he came back, at twenty-two years old, the third of five children, to manage Tresco. He has two sons and one daughter and has recently married his second wife, Lucy.

the quays and all the things that go with an island. Two years ago we installed a sewage system because we realized that, in spite of all the things politicians say on TV, there is absolutely no commitment whatsoever to cleaning anything up. The Government wouldn't give us any financial help, but we did it anyway. It was hellish expensive but it's good.

If you talk to people on the other islands, they'll say you can't work on Tresco, the whole thing's a dictatorship. But the other side of it is that there's more security here even though people have service contracts. If you have a cottage which is maintained and insured and a regular job, as happens here, then it's an economic concern. And you know that if you've been here a reasonable amount of time, we'll provide you with a house to retire in, rent free, and we don't charge locals to keep a boat in the harbour.

I don't see the possibility of more people permanently resident here because the indigenous industries have more or less petered out. We've increased the number of jobs in Tresco in the last twenty years because we've gone on finding new services to offer. But there must be a limit to this. We don't want more visitors in the gardens which are the jewel in the crown – they would detract from the pleasure of visiting. We have a landing charge which started about 1960 as a fund for maintaining the quays, but it's also a means of control. If you quadrupled the number of visitors, we'd feel the pressure to a point where it would lose a lot of its charm. I know there's the danger of aiming for somewhere to be preserved in aspic – we always have to keep our eyes open to opportunity, not in terms of increasing numbers of people or buildings, but in terms of increasing the quality of life. What we want is a living community and the means to support it, and so far I think we've succeeded.

I'm always wide open to a number of charges. One is that I'm going to over-develop the island. But I live here most of the time and am very conscious of its significance. It's the last of a breed – there aren't many islands that haven't been destroyed. There really aren't. When people talk about development or change, everything is relative and I know how precious the peace and quiet of this place is – there are no private cars and every vehicle you see on the road is geared to running the island.

The only thing that really gets up my nose is the people who say I've destroyed the community by making the island self-sufficient. It's such a contradiction of everything I've ever tried to do. I don't respond any more. One of the things you learn in life is that if you respond to everyone who snipes at you, you exhaust yourself and it makes no difference in the end. You have to have confidence about running a place like this and in your own decisions. I obviously take advice from all directions, but at the end of the day, someone has to make the decision and in Tresco's case, it has to be me.

THE HEAD GARDENER/ASSISTANT AIR TRAFFIC CONTROLLER

This is one of the top private gardens in Britain because of the wide range of plants – we probably have the best collection from the southern hemisphere growing outside in Britain because it doesn't get cold in winter. The garden isn't planted like a typical British garden – we don't have borders and straight edges. I think there's a Mediterranean feel about it with a hint of South Africa and Australia thrown in, and you don't have to be a gardener to enjoy it – you come round a corner and there's the 'ooh aah' factor – big palm trees, lots of exotic succulents in flower.

We have about 3,000 different species and a national collection of Acacias with 68 kinds, and 50 or 60 Eucalyptus. We're always planting. At the moment, we're doing our wind-breaks and putting in nearly five thousand Monterey Cyprus and pine trees a year – the kind Augustus Smith, the chap who started the gardens, planted. There's nothing here older than 150 years because when he came in the 1830s there were no trees at all, but he built a wall to cut out the wind and planted some behind it and they grew. Wind

Mike Nelham, thirty-seven, trained at the Royal Horticultural Garden at Wisley, Surrey, has a National Diploma in Horticulture, and came to the Abbey Gardens on a scholarship in 1976. He worked at High Beeches in Sussex and in 1984, at twenty-six, returned to Tresco as Head Gardener. He is married to Isabel, whose family have been here for three generations, and they have two daughters.

protection and shelter are the key to everything here. In 1990 we had a hurricane that blew all the wind-breaks over. But this could have been the best thing to happen because they were very old and would have had to come down anyway.

When the cruise liners are here we have to organize their arrival with the boatmen and often give 150 passengers a guided tour at 7.30 a.m. before the garden is open. I probably go on three or four trips a year to find plants, and to Gardeners' Guild and Institute of Horticulture meetings. I encourage my gardeners to chat with people and don't think we get many plants taken – if people want something, we'll gladly give them a cutting – I'd much rather have that than someone rip a lump off something.

Today, at 1 o'clock, I'm running the heliport. The helicopter comes in twice a day from Penzance, three times from July to September, and lands 40 yd from the garden gate. I'm the assistant air traffic controller and deputy heliport manager and many of the gardeners are trained firemen and first-aiders.

I get rung up at night from all sorts of people saying they've read about the gardens and could I give them advice about their own. Some think we shouldn't charge much for plants and it's difficult to put across that these days all expenses have to be taken into consideration. I have an annual budget which comes from our thirty thousand visitors and a few plant sales, and it has to cover the cost of six to seven gardeners, their housing, machinery, compost, seeds, travel and materials.

I know I'll find it very difficult to leave, but I won't stay on the island when I retire. Lurking round in the background wouldn't be good for me – better to let the new man start with a clean sheet.

Derek Tabron, forty-five, taught at a private school in Kenya and worked in teacher education at Nottingham Polytechnic before coming to Scilly in 1990. He is now the Head Teacher of Tresco (Church of England controlled) Primary School, which has thirty-three chldren. He is married to Hilary, and they have three children.

THE HEAD TEACHER

The main part of the building goes back to Victorian times and we have two classes: four- to seven-year-olds, and seven- to eleven-year-olds, and two teachers. There was a bit of a scare when the Government started talking about surplus places, but we think we're safe at the moment. There used to be a school on Bryher but that was closed down when they got to about two children, so now they all come over here every day by boat. Sometimes they're a bit late, but it's only very occasionally they don't get across. If the weather forecast is bad and it's blowing up, I send them home early.

The parents here are marvellous from the support point of view. We had our May Day yesterday and you only have to tell one person about it, and suddenly there's a whole spread of food and drink there. If I have to ask for books or information from home, there's no trouble at all. We get so many visitors on Tresco and when we have our summer fête we can easily make £1,000. That's a lot of buying power for Tresco school and we make other money throughout the year. Recently we've spent it on computer equipment; my predecessor spent money on musical instruments – we keep trying to do recorders, but because I teach all the time and some children come from Bryher, it makes organizing this very difficult. Out-of-school activities just don't exist or if they do, you immediately cut out all the Bryher children. At one time they used to go to Tresco homes for lunch, but as the numbers grew that got more difficult to arrange and now they go to the New Inn, and pay what they would if they were in any other school. It caused a bit of amusement at first. I think the *Daily Mirror* did an article on it.

THE HOTELIER

When the hotel is at full steam, we have seventy-five guests and thirty-eight staff. Visitors have to be fairly fit, because there isn't any transport, but elderly people can use our golf buggies if they want to, and if someone needs to go to the Abbey Gardens, we'll run them down on the hotel bus which is a tractor with a covered trailer and cushioned seating. We've had a few golf writers at the hotel who feel if there was a golf-course here it would be one of the most

Ivan Curtis, thirty-two, lived abroad for much of his childhood, studied catering management, owned a pub in Telford, worked in hotels for eleven years (including the Queens in Eastbourne, the Metropole and Grand in Brighton). He came to Scilly as general manager at The Island Hotel in 1991. He is married to Sue, and they have three children.

unique in the world. But I don't want one. I'm quite happy to go to St Mary's for that.

When we're interviewing for staff, we always try to put them off – we don't tell them anything that's good about the hotel or the island – the brochure does that. We tell them precisely what's wrong with the place: there are no night-clubs, no discos, no Macdonalds. It's a place where you have to be creative in your own mind in your time off – you can't get in the car and speed up the motorway for a couple of hundred miles to burn the energy off. You're stuck here. Invariably, as soon as you say there's no night club, they say, 'Stop, we're not interested.' I had six people within five minutes saying it wasn't the place for them, but you have to be truthful.

Sue helps in the hotel, cleans the school – on Tresco you do a bit of everything – and organizes the play group. She feels she's doing something for the children which is worthwhile. They are the central part of the community, the future.

THE GALLERY CO-MANAGER

Lucy Dorrien Smith, thirty-three, was brought up in an art gallery home in Newlyn, Cornwall, where her parents were the curators. She was a nurse for eight years, worked on yachts round the world, and is now co-manager of an art gallery on Tresco which opened in April 1992 in an old boat-house built in the First World War for seaplanes. She married Robert Dorrien Smith in 1993.

I have exhibitions for many local artists and if I like the work of those from other parts of the country, I write and ask if they'd like to visit Tresco. There's a cottage we set aside a week or two a month and they come with their families, on their own, or with another artist, writer, or photographer and take their inspiration from the islands. They paint, make tapestries or pot, then go home and work up for an exhibition usually the following year.

We have water-colours from £35 to £80, and oil paintings from £350 to £4,000. That one over there costs about £8,000. We don't sell many of the higher priced ones, but we do one or two. We've gathered potters from St Mary's and St Martin's, etchers from Bryher, and sell belts, bags and satchels made from Russian reindeer leather found in a ship wrecked off Plymouth in 1750. Guy Lock, who lives on St Mary's, makes tables and chairs and lamp stands from wreck wood and trees blown down in the storm.

THE QUAY SHOPKEEPER

It's more commercial here than it used to be. In lots of places I'd like to put the clock back, but it's the same wherever you live, home's home, isn't it? We always used to get the same people coming back each year, but as the years go by they get older and it probably gets too much to come. I remember when Henry Bond, the butler at the Abbey, used to meet them from the boat with a horse and cart.

This shop was once a shed for parcels from the cargo boat, but it wasn't as big as it is now, I think they tacked a piece on. I sell the odd thing like baked beans and snacks, and biscuits and crisps, but I don't do much in the food line. I have cups of tea for people waiting for the boat and they can sit at that large table there. In the summer we get a lot of requests for newspapers and I have to mark them all up and people come and get them. There's all sorts come here, but no royalty this year – they always come here when they come over. It's quite nice in winter. You get the odd gale, and some cold winds, depending on the direction, of course. I'm open but we don't get a lot of people after November.

Gloria Lawry, sixty-three, was born on Tresco – her grandfather had come as a coastguard. She went to school on the island, worked at the New Inn, and twenty years ago took over the shop on the quay which she now rents from the Tresco Estate. She is a widow and has seven grandchildren. Her son-in-law is Head Gardener at the Abbey Gardens.

ST MARTIN'S

St Martin's, the third largest of the islands and the most north-easterly, is a narrow ridge of land about 2 miles long, with cliffs on the rugged north coast and small enclosed flower fields leading down to long white sandy beaches on the south. In the east is the Daymark, built as a daylight navigational aid in 1683 (not 1637 as inscribed). In 1989 a granite statue, believed to be over three thousand years old and the oldest in Britain, was re-erected. There are landing quays at both ends of the island.

A concrete road (made by the islanders) leads from Higher Town through Middle Town to Lower Town, though the word 'town' is rather a misnomer – the only buildings are a scattering of houses for the ninety people who live here, a post office stores, a church, a school, the Seven Stones pub, a tea room, self-catering cottages, guest-houses and a twenty-four bedroom single storey luxury hotel opened in 1989.

The best way to see what else the island has to offer is to walk up from the quay at Higher Town and read the signposts at the top of the lane: bird-watching; fishing trips; a Sailing and Diving Centre; crafts and outdoor gear at Glenmore Cottage shop; an art gallery, and Little Arthur Farm run on self-sufficiency principles.

There are lovely walks along the cliffs where purple heather and golden gorse grow, and if it's windy on one side of the island, you can find shelter on the other. In the evenings visitors are welcome to join in the whist drives, country dances, folk nights, and slide shows in the Reading Room. From Easter to October there's a daily boat service to other islands and from early May, evening trips to watch the gig races.

THE CROFTER

My main source of income is small boat fishing – shellfish and grey mullet, which I sell locally whenever possible. If you put fish on the open market, you have to buy ice, pay freight and harbour dues, and are totally at the mercy of the buyers. I keep a few cattle, keep the land tidy. I used to do milk, but there are so many rules and regulations now courtesy of Europe, God help us, that I stopped. During the winter, I pick flowers.

Grey mullet can come in very close, when the tide's nearly high water, and the wind is beating on the shore. They like rough water and they're magic fish to watch – the longer you hunt them, the greater respect and interest you have for them. Sometimes you can be looking at a patch of water and you know they're there but you can't see them. And then suddenly they just spring into focus, it's just like switching a light on and there they are, and you see them coming along with their heads up out of the water, they roll over on their back and there's a flash of silver as they do it. Normally, as soon as it's fit to get there with a boat, they move off and you can't catch them. But it gives you an idea of the quantity that are around and it's fascinating to watch them anyway – it's also wonderful to catch them as they're worth about £3.50 each.

A bit later in the year, you're looking for shoals of pilchards – when they're massed up and spawning there are red patches in the water. When you see them, I don't know how many thousands, you understand the word biomass because there is just this great wodge of fish and then suddenly they'll all turn together and the whole water will be silver. Then they're gone and as they go down, you drift net for them.

Archaeology has been a hobby of mine for forty years and I give a once-a-week lecture on the history of Scilly. It

Keith Low, forty-seven, a Scillonian, went to school in Truro, worked in child care for Wandsworth Borough Council, and at twenty-one became deputy superintendent at a Cornwall Education Department children's home. In 1968 he decided to make his living in Scilly. He is divorced, and has two daughters.

gives people another aspect of things they would normally walk past – burial chambers, Bronze Age field systems, hut circles and field systems under the sea from when Scilly was one island. When I was seven, a professor was excavating on Tean and my uncle took me over one evening to see what was going on. I started asking questions, and this important man actually stopped work and showed me around. That was a real object lesson to me because I've realized ever since that if you want to get people interested in things, catch them when they're young. Today I go fishing, there are children on the quay, they want to know what you're doing, I give them a bit of bait. Look after the children, that's the future for Scilly.

SCHOOLTEACHER

Heather Terry, forty-seven, attended St Martin's Primary School as a pupil, as did her father and grandfather and she has taught both her children here. She trained at Westminster College, near Oxford, taught on the mainland for eight years, is married to Alan, a house decorator and boatman. The school has seven children and she is the only teacher.

People sometimes think teaching seven children from four to eleven is an easy option, but I find it as demanding as a mainland school because although you don't have the stress of a lot of children waiting for guidance or help, you do have that wide ability stretch. It's a long time to keep the same group motivated and their enthusiasm going. And of course the relationship between teacher and child has got to be right because they're not going to change teacher in September.

At present I have five boys and two girls full-time, but it fluctuates. We've been down to as few as three and still kept going. Next year we're going to take quite a blow because three of them move on to secondary education, but I think we're safer than on the mainland where children can be bussed to school, because here, there's that bit of water to cross.

I've got two rooms. This is the academic one, for want of a better word, and that's the practical one with PE apparatus, TV, two computers and a sink. How do I interest older and younger children at the same time? I try to balance it between those doing their bread and butter work, mathematics and language at their own level, and then – so that we don't fall into seven separate little units that can become like the loneliness of the long distance textbook – we try to take a project which I can bring us all into. This term, we're doing ancient and modern Egypt because it fits into the National Curriculum history and geography. I plan what we hope to cover, take core tasks that we do together, aurally possibly, and then hive off other activities to suit age or ability. It seems to work reasonably well.

We begin each day with an assembly, then start the ball rolling with maths and English. Sometimes we have science and I use TV and radio programmes to broaden their outlook. We're well catered for and children do seem to thrive and progress because of the small numbers and family atmosphere. Organized games are difficult, of course, but they have quite a physical life on the island, and we have the sea and the use of the hotel pool.

By the time they get to eleven, they're looking for a wider sphere of friends – there are very few choices of friendship here. If you have a squabble with someone in the playground, it's not easy to go off and find another group. We try to break them in gently for going to secondary school on St Mary's – they have a couple of nights at the hostel there, visit the school, and the teachers come here to get to know them.

Parents all help and support anything I do, and if we put on a play or a show, they turn up. If I go to a social function, they don't talk to me about their children, and when I send a letter regarding something in school to parents who are my friends, I always put 'Dear Mr and Mrs', rather than their Christian names. It's just to make a division and people have respected it.

It was always my dream to come back and not everyone is able to fulfil their dreams. I think I'm the only Scillonian woman back in Scilly doing what this Authority trained me to do. While most want to get back, they probably have to forsake their career to do so, and men have to go for fishing, boats or tourism. I just hope the school can keep going for the sake of the islands.

I love the relationship I build up with the children. I have the satisfaction of seeing the continuity of all their primary school development, something you can't do at a mainland school. I think all except one of those who have been here longer than two terms have done 'A' Levels, and that one exception is now doing an engineering degree. And you think, well, it is working. As long as the relationship is right, everything seems to slot into place.

THE SUB-POSTMISTRESS

Daphne Perkins, sixty-five, came to Scilly at the age of twelve in the second year of the war when her father was a coastguard, and has been here ever since. She became sub-postmistress twenty-seven years ago and now runs the post office and stores. Her brother, Terry, does the delivering and runs the local boat.

I left school at fourteen – there was no such thing as taking exams to get away then. Mum took the post office over when I was fifteen so I've been here about fifty years – it sounds awful when you think about it. When we first came, we only had mail in and out three times a week – the steamer would come one day and go back – but these last few years, the post goes across to the mainland by helicopter, so we get mail in and out every day. We used to get it from the quay with a pony and cart and it's gradually got to tractors and vans. Everyone's got one or the other, but only two people have cars. My brother brings all the stuff for the shop – it comes in big containers which they off-load from the launch on to the tractor and we unload it straight into the garage.

The first thing I do in the morning is to change the date stamp. There's much more mail to be hand-stamped now and I must have done thousands of cards and letters in a year, but it's good for the muscles! Then I sweep up and do the ordering to St Mary's because they've got to get everything packed up and over to us in the launch that day. I sell a lot of food stuffs and all the basic things, and John Goddard at the pub deals with the newspapers. Years ago, when we just had the steamer, we only got papers three times a week. W.H. Smith in Penzance used to bundle them all up with everyone's names on them, and we had to go down to the quay and sort them all out. If you ordered a Sunday paper, you'd get Sunday, Monday and Tuesday's all on Tuesday. But we didn't have television so you hadn't seen anything, though you might have heard the news on the radio.

I have Jenny to help me in the shop now and Judy comes in when I need her from about Easter to Whitsun, and on what we call bread days. We have bread from St Mary's three times a week, you see, and you have to order it the day before from the Kavorna Bakery. Sometimes it's a real nightmare in the summer months trying to work out how much we want. This weekend there were about 30 large white, so many small ones, in-the-teens of large wholemeal uncut, about 30 wholemeal sliced, and up to about 20 white sliced. Then there's the granary and the champion. It can get up to over a hundred loaves three times a week. But there's not much profit out of bread really. You sell it hoping people will buy something else. Some self-catering visitors bring things with them, but a lot will send a grocery order to us in advance. It's handy for them on a Saturday night, specially if the boat's late.

In the winter, we're only more or less ourselves unless anyone comes for Christmas. I tie flowers for my brother who has a flower farm – he brings them for me to do in the mail room, because I'm up there for hours and nobody comes to the shop. In the evenings, we have whist drives that I like to go to, though they're not held so often now since the television. At one time we had one every Saturday, but we have been having country dancing down at the pub once a fortnight.

I'm trying to make up my mind what to do when I retire. Am I going to stay here or go? I think I've decided to stay. I'd miss the sea, and if you go somewhere else, you don't know people the same as you do here.

THE OFF-ISLAND COUNCILLOR

One of our big problems is the lack of affordable houses for youngsters wanting to live here – there are no council houses on the off-islands. I think it's time the Council went in with the Duchy to make more available so young couples

Colin Daly, fifty-six, an industrial chemist, has lived on St Martin's for twenty years and has a small flower farm. He is a Royal Yachting Association-approved sailing instructor, an auxiliary coastguard, and was the prime mover in bringing mains electricity to the off-islands. He was recently elected to the Isles of Scilly Council, is married to Steve, a keen herb grower, and they have one son.

can start families and keep the community going. There are quite a lot of redundant farm buildings and if tenants were willing to give them up, the Duchy could convert them into small starter homes. They'd also be suitable for older people to live in after their families leave. I think this is a good idea, but it can be a bit surprising to people on St Mary's who view the off-islands as a theme park for their visitors to go to, and tend to resist changing them. It will take a bit of convincing to get them to move.

How did I get the electricity to the off-islands? In the late '70s St Mary's had a power-station that produced its own electricity, but we only had small generators on the off-islands. I thought there must be some legislation about electricity, so when I was in London, I decided to read through the Acts of Parliament in a library and HM Stationery Office. I unearthed what I wanted in an Act of 1899. It said that six or more premises along a road could put a requisition to their local Board, and the Board had to lay on electricity. I tried not to jump up in the air shouting Eureka, but I had an internal yippee because I realized this was the way we were going to get it.

That was in 1981. We held lots of public meetings and the vast majority were in favour. The Board challenged our requisition at first, but we came to an agreement that we would pay £1,000 per connection. The work began in 1982, laying the submarine cables to St Mary's and cabling up all the islands. We were determined it should be underground, so it wouldn't spoil the scenery. The Duchy were very good about this – they helped us with a sum of money and a firm instruction from Prince Charles that he didn't want over-head power lines. We were actually switched on in 1985 and had an official ceremony by Prince Charles in 1986.

We then had a second campaign to get the same tariff as the rest of the country – we were charged a lot extra for our electricity because it was being generated by diesel on St Mary's. In the end they laid a cable from the mainland to Scilly, so we're now part of the national grid and have the same price electricity as anywhere else.

One thing I haven't mentioned at all is this thing called

the environment. It's like everywhere else: what do we do with our rubbish? Starting this autumn, it's going to St Mary's, which sounds like we're exporting the problem, but they're sending separated aluminium and iron tins to the mainland for recycling. The glass will be crushed here and used instead of gravel for making cement for building. No sewerage goes into the sea now, we all have septic tanks. Cars used to be thrown over the cliff, but there's a new boat with a big crane on it, and anything that can be got to the quay – old cars or tractors – is taken away free of charge.

THE YOUNG SCILLONIAN

I started part-time school here when I was about four years old and stayed until I was eleven. At first there were over ten of us, but in my last term there was just my brother, the teacher's daughter and me. It was nice being so few, you got much more individual attention, but it was quite a big step going to St Mary's at eleven.

We took the boat there every Monday morning at about 8 a.m., and stayed at the boarding house until Friday. I didn't find it too bad. In fact, I quite enjoyed it most of the time. Some people get homesick, specially on Monday morning, but after a while you think you've got to go, so you might as well make the most of it. There were times when the tides were very high, and we had to wait for them to go down from the quay. We sometimes came home at 10 or 11 a.m. if they thought the weather was going to get worse.

In the summer at the hostel you're allowed out until quarter of an hour before your bedtime, depending on where you are going. In the winter you're allowed out as long as you're going to friends, but you have to be in by 9 p.m. There's a café we'd go to, and the Scillonian Club, which you can go to once you're fifteen. In the winter it gets quite boring because there aren't a lot of things to do. But once you get to the fourth or fifth year, you don't really seem to have time to go out because of the course work.

Louise Walder, sixteen, was born on St Mary's. Both sides of her family have lived in Scilly for many generations and her parents have a farm and a fishing boat. She has just taken her GCSEs and is going to college on the mainland to do 'A' Levels. She has a younger brother.

You want to do it during the week, because then you have time at the weekend to spend with your family, or go out.

The school has a big range of activities for such a small one – sailing, canoeing, cookery, textiles, conservation, trampolining; many pupils go to Cornwall to compete in judo, and football matches. Teachers try their best for us to have things to do. I was a manager from the third year and in the fifth a senior manager. We organized social activities and tried to improve things. We also tried to get feedback from people in the school about what they wanted. I don't know any other school that does this, I think it was Mr Howell's idea. He decided he wanted some communication between pupils, teachers and governors. I enjoy organizing things!

I am ready for a change now. Living over here is so different, even different to Penzance. There's so much more to do there, like the cinema and the shops. And I have a lot of relations there. I think I'd like to do a teacher training course, I've always wanted to work with children, but I'll have to have a good think about it first.

THE PUBLICAN

Edna Goddard, fifty-seven, who came from Tresco, runs the Sevenstones pub, with her husband, John, a former Isles of Scilly councillor for twenty-five years, and daughter, Mandy. They also have two sons working on the island.

We were flower farmers until twenty years ago, and then felt that if our three children wanted to come back to Scilly after they'd done their schooling there wasn't enough here for them. We thought as there was no public house that it would be nice to have one, and we threw ourselves in at the deep end and built one from our stables and garage. Of course, we had to get Duchy permission but it went through okay seeing there hadn't been a pub here for sixty years, and I think that was just someone's sitting-room with barrels of beer and spirits.

I say we're a pub, but we're a community centre really, because children come in and we sell lots of soft drinks, specially in the summer. It's always been seasonal, and in the winter we used to tell people we were here and if anyone wanted the pub open, we'd open on demand. But they never liked to knock us up. Now with the hotel round the corner these last four years, we stay open every other night in winter and for Sunday lunch as well.

On an average summer night we get about fifty or sixty people and sometimes have a live band. On an evening like that, we have about a hundred customers – my garden goes for a burton, they're all dancing out there, but they enjoy it, it's a lovely night.

THE FLOWERS-BY-POST PEOPLE

Hilary and Andrew Julian are both Cornish but spent twenty years in London until seven years ago they came to live in Scilly. Andrew was a police inspector in Brixton and had spent holidays on St Martin's, Hilary was a teacher. Now they run a flower farm, holiday lets, and a 'Scent by Post' business. They have two grown-up children.

Andrew: How did we learn about flower farming? We persuaded the previous tenant to let us come here to work for nothing if we could have free accommodation, and we picked up a lot in that first year. Being at school in Truro helped because many of the flower farmers are old Truronians, so I could phone them and say, 'Help, what do I do with this?' We had a lot of very good advice and, of course, you read and learn. At first, we found it very frustrating that we couldn't get what we wanted immediately as we had in London. People would say things like, 'Well, I expect such and such a thing will be up tomorrow, boy.' Your life does become ruled by weather and tides, but you do learn to slow down. You get used to a changing pace of life which is dictated by forces beyond your control, but it's taken us a year or two to do it.

Hilary: We started the flowers-by-post five years ago on a very small scale. With prices getting more and more depressed, we felt there was a need to market flowers in a way that would give us a better return and enable us to keep the farm running the way we want to. We'd also like to find flowers from other farmers – islanders have to look somewhere to market them with so many foreign imports. In the last eight months, we've sent two thousand postal boxes and are aiming for five thousand by the end of the year. I'm eventually aiming for a hundred thousand.

Andrew: Do I do any police work here? You don't need policemen if you've got a community.

THE HOTEL MANAGER

Michael Bryant, thirty-nine, worked in the hotel trade in Africa, Majorca, Cornwall and Devon, ran a restaurant in St Ives, and came to the St Martin's Hotel in 1990, a year after it was built. He is married and has three children at school on the island.

The hotel was built to look like a cluster of cottages overlooking the long sandy beach, by Cornish hotelier Robert Francis for whom, as he said, a dream became a reality, but it was a reality that couldn't be afforded. It cost too much to build in the first place and interest rates just got out of hand. It was rescued from receivership by Peter Sykes, a semi-retired businessman from Bristol, and it has certainly brought employment to the island. There are now four couples here who weren't before – the island could stagnate if we didn't have that influx of young people.

In fact, the hotel has just won an Egon Ronay award for looking after children. We don't have a lot of facilities but if there are quite a few here we lay on things like swimming galas and treasure hunts, and take them off parents' hands for a day. Last year we took a crowd in a boat to the island over there – they had proper maps and found buried treasure in the form of sweets. We also do corporate and incentive programmes which we sell overseas and I do these Treasure Island events for them too – we take guests off to uninhabited islands and they have to build rafts and solve clues on maps. We have a lot of fun doing them.

BRYHER

Bryher, meaning 'land of the hills', is 1 mile long, 1½ miles wide and the smallest of the inhabited islands. The east coast is sheltered and only a five minute boat ride or fifteen minute walk across the sand at low tide to Tresco, to which it was once joined. The west coast is rocky and lashed by giant Atlantic seas; the south has sandy beaches and safe bathing.

There is archaeological evidence of life here from Neolithic times until AD 500 and on Shipman Head Down, prehistoric boulder walls run criss-cross over the moorland. Here at night, in the spring and summer months, you can hear the Manx Shearwaters as they swoop over the cliffs making their eerie calls in the windy darkness.

A report of 1579 shows the island was suitable for twenty people and by 1796 there were eleven families. Kelping (burning seaweed for making soap and glass) was the main source of livelihood. But in the 1830s clergy from Penzance found islanders had turned yellow from eating nothing but limpets, and every tree and bush had been burnt for fuel.

Today there is a population of eighty-three, a post office and general store, one hotel, two cafés, four guest-houses, one camp site and self-catering cottages. Oil lamps hang from the beams in the eighteenth-century church (electric light and gas heating tucked discreetly away) and the graveyard in spring is perfumed by flowers known as three-cornered leeks, which look like white bluebells and smell of garlic. There are no roads, but rough tracks where wild flowers grow on the verges beneath low stone walls.

Bryher's boat service functions all the year round and in 1991, helped by Anneka Rice's television programme and a lot of effort from local people, a new low water jetty was built.

THE OLDEST MAN ON BRYHER

There were about sixteen or seventeen pupils when I was at school here. That dwindled until there were only three, and then they closed the school down. At the end of term the Town Clerk came up to Father, I can see him now, we were making lobster pots at the time. 'Charlie, your boy has got to go to Tresco after Easter.' And I can hear Father saying, 'Well, Mr Boyle, my son is not going to Tresco after Easter.' I was thirteen and a half and I never went to school no more. I was pleased, although I must admit, I did get on at school alright.

Once I'd have liked to be somewhere on the mainland but as things are now, we often say to each other, we're glad we live in this little quiet corner. I always think of Father saying, 'We get rough days and we get fine days, and the fine days outnumber the rough ones.' You've seen Cromwell's Castle? The wind can pick up the sea and drop it in at the top and it runs out the windows each side. The headland at Bryher can be buried completely out of sight, and Scilly Rock too.

It's very different here from what it used to be. We had a meeting yesterday with Council officials about the sea defences. Oh dear. I'm the only one now that knows what it used to be like, if you understand my meaning. I could tell them when the sea wall was built in 1923, and the Duchy of Cornwall told us to dump all the trees, old stone, any old thing on to the banks to catch the sand. And they planted marram grass and the banks came up. But the Council has now had surveys done and how much do you think they want to do the sea defences in Scilly? £18 million. It's ridiculous. They want to spend over £1 million on Bryher with a 75 per cent grant if it's finalized, but Bryher and the Council have to find the rest and how are we going to find that amount of money? I rather told them, in no uncertain

Leonard Jenkins, seventy-six, was born on Bryher, has lived here all his life and has a family tree that goes back to 1600. He was in the Navy during the war, farmed and fished until he was about fifty, then started a passenger boat service which his son, Ken, now carries on. He is married to Elizabeth Ann.

terms, to scrap the whole lot. They could have spent about £9,000 and done the job, but what annoyed me is that they had already spent £25,000 on the survey. The Council said no and I'm glad they did. But it would have been better if they'd contacted local people first.

I don't know why I like living here, but there's something that attracts you and keeps you. I'd like to see more of the land brought back into cultivation like it used to be. It grieves me to see the farms now. I've worked on every one of them – there were about twenty and only five today – and when September came twenty years ago, it was a picture. All the bulbs had been planted, the grass cleaned up, all black ground, all the fences in trim – it looked, well, like a garden.

THE OFF-ISLAND COUNCILLOR

Marian Bennett, forty-five, came to Bryher on holiday when she was about six and knew this was the place she wanted to live. Her parents moved here when they retired, and in 1973 she married Keith and they have two children. In 1980 she was elected to the Isles of Scilly Council. She was Chairman of the Tourist Board for eight years and is now Chairman of the Airport and Transport Committee.

Getting to Council meetings involves ordering a boat to take us to St Mary's, setting off about an hour before the meeting, and often arriving with seaweed hanging out of my sandals. You develop techniques for looking smart: a good hair spray, waterproof mascara, high heels made of patent rather than leather which shows the salt marks. In fact, I often unthinkingly put on a tight skirt that makes getting on and off boats totally impractical, and visitors tend to look askance when they see someone tripping down the quay, high heels, tight skirt, smart jacket. They nudge each other and say, 'You can tell she doesn't live here.'

I'll never forget the time we got the new quay. The island had wanted a low tide access one for years – we'd got European and Royal Development Commission money, but could never quite manage the shortfall which came to several thousands of pounds. You just can't do that with a population of seventy-odd. Then I saw the programme *Challenge Anneka* and thought I'd try that. Researchers came down, but every time there was some very good reason why they couldn't undertake the project. The main problem was the amount of aggregates needed for the quay top. Finally, Keith said, 'Why don't you put a wooden top on?' and the engineer said, 'What a good idea.' And they went ahead. It was a wonderful project because the whole island joined in and at three or four in the morning, we were down on the beach, thigh deep in wet sand, plastering these piers and all singing under the broadwalk, a very unlikely combination of islanders all working together.

One thing I'm very keen to see implemented is for the *Scillonian* to be subsidized because it is the lifeline link to the islands and we'd never be able to manage without it. I feel we should be treated in the same ways as some of the Scottish islands are.

THE DIVER

Nothing I'd been taught to do would possibly have been any use in Scilly and people thought it was a horrendous decision to come. At first we lived on a boat and in holiday lets in the winter and I got a job as a boatman for a small diving crew working on historic wrecks. Every day the divers would disappear from my sight for half an hour and then they'd come up and I'd sort the things they'd brought up. It became a driving force for me to get down there and see what it was like. It was *The Hollandia*, a Dutch Eastern ship of 1743, that got me interested in treasure diving. She went down with fifty thousand pieces of eight and we've brought up thirty-eight thousand of them.

I realized that the basic thing I needed for this type of work was a specialized craft. So I designed a boat, had it built and started on my own as a diver in 1988. Now I work to order: quay repairs, sewage pipe extensions, moorings, any work that requires diving. Certain vessels have gone down with defined cargo and I negotiate with the owners and salvage it. I dismantle Victorian steamship engines for bronze and white metal, copper and lead piping, and sell them to scrap metal merchants. We've found pieces of pottery going back to 200 or 300 BC but that was from the wreck of the *Collusus,* which went down in 1708 carrying

Mac Mace, fifty, from Nottinghamshire, was self-employed in the packaging industry when in 1975 he came to Scilly with his wife, Tracy, and their two children.

some of Sir William Hamilton's (husband of Emma) collection of Etruscan pottery.

There's no dive that doesn't have that wonderful hope and anticipation about it, because basically you're somewhere where not many other people have had a chance to look. A ship is a package containing an assortment of things that made up life on that ship at the moment of time it ceased: all the day-to-day items used on board, nails that held the timber together, knives, forks, cups and saucers, the medicine chest, the surgeons' and navigators' instruments, all those are in this packet which has disintegrated, and if you dig long enough you'll find bits and pieces. Most shipwrecks, in fact about 90 per cent, are not wrecks, they're just sites where wrecks happened, and they're the really interesting ones.

THE HOTELIER

Sorrel Atkinson, forty-one, an artist, ran an art gallery in Sandwich, Kent, and her husband, James, was a pilot in the Merchant Navy before they bought Hell Bay Hotel. They have four children.

I wouldn't want to be a hotelier on the mainland, but I just fell for the island, which was strange because I'm frightened of the sea and don't like flying. But I feel so at home here, it's uncanny. My husband who went to sea when he was seventeen and has always travelled, says it's like living on a big ship that doesn't go anywhere.

There's a limited number of people here so you have to fall back on your own resources a bit. I've been bar maid, chambermaid, laundrymaid, painter and decorator at the hotel though I haven't actually cooked a meal yet. Of course we are very dependent on the tides, and the channel (between Bryher and Tresco) dries out, so that one day we could have a hundred lunches and another day ten, depending whether the boats have come up. One thing you learn is to be patient, there's no point getting in a fuss when you're stuck on St Mary's with only half an hour's shopping to do and a four hour wait for the boat. You just have a cup of coffee and . . . wait. You see people arriving on holiday fairly stressed out: 'Why isn't the boat here? We can't possibly wait half an hour.' But that's just not the way we live over here.

But you can have problems. We've been renovating part of the building and waiting and waiting for the windows to arrive. They came – and all the wrong size. But because they'd taken two months to get here, we made the holes slightly bigger or smaller and just got on with it. You can't go banging on the builders' door and saying this is no good. You haven't got any clout. And for supplies, you have to think two weeks ahead all the time, you can't nip round the corner if you've run out of something.

A year after we moved in, someone said, 'Well, I suppose you've come here to find yourself', but you have to have found yourself before you end up in a place like this. We're really like a big family on Bryher. It's not always happy but you rub along. Some people you like better than others, but you know jolly well if there's a crisis, everyone will pull together. There are always a couple of parties at Christmas that everybody's invited to, a carol service for the children and they go out carol singing. New Year's Eve we often have an island party where everyone produces dishes. We've tried a disco, but we're a bit short on teenagers. My four all went to Tresco school and I used to walk to the boat with them. One of the questions they get asked from visitors is, 'Isn't it exciting to go to school by boat?' and they roll their eyes and say, 'Not again!' [laughs].

THE POSTWOMAN

I start the day at 7 a.m. and go and milk my goats. Then I get the mail – there's not usually that much and I can get most of it on my bike. It comes to St Mary's on the first helicopter from the mainland, but that doesn't mean it will come straight up here to Bryher because of the tide – it can really arrive any time. It comes every day, and I have to collect and sort it each day, but I only deliver on Monday, Wednesday and Friday, and that takes about an hour and a half. There are only two letter-boxes, and I knock on all the other doors, open them, and put the post inside. None of the

Rosalie Tildesley, fifty-two, a former nursery nurse, comes from Kent and has lived in Scilly for twenty-six years. She is married to Mike.

locals lock them. I see most people every day if they're in, but I'm not always first with island news and am quite surprised to hear things I haven't discovered.

I'm the co-owner of a donkey and a pony, we grow some vegetables, and have a cow that my husband looks after. We sell the goat's milk to local people and visitors in the summer. It's very nice, virtually without cream and very digestible. If I have any extra, I occasionally make cheese. In the summer I clean the public toilets down by the quay and on Sunday I cook at Fraggle Rock Café because that's the chef's day off.

THE BOAT BUILDERS

Keith Bennett, sixty-two, trained as a model-maker, did his National Service in the section that made models for the Dambuster raids, became a medical instrument maker, and, arriving in Scilly in 1957 in a 17 ft catamaran, decided to stay. He is now a member of the Environmental Trust, is married to Marian and they have two children.

Keith Bennett: About 1960 someone asked me if I could build a boat, then there was another one, and before I knew where I was, I was building them the whole time. I started in someone's pigsty which the Duchy found out about, thought they'd better offer me a building and I went from pigsty to cowshed.

I like making catamarans. I'm interested in the fact that they are different, and they're all timber. I don't go in for fibreglass, not because I don't like working with it or because it's no good, but because I just don't want to be poisoned by fumes and die young. The biggest catamaran I've made was 36 ft long. The last big one we built was 32 ft long and would cost about £40,000 today, but we do little dinghies for just under £600. I only make to order, perhaps two a year. It's difficult to get anyone to help you. You can't just advertise for a shipwright, there's nowhere for them to live, so you have to have casual labour when you can get it. I made the local coastguard boat, and one for a French count, the grandson of Ferdinand de Lessops, the Suez Canal builder. You get all sorts of odd characters who turn up wanting boats.

Working on the Environmental Trust is quite difficult as the Trust lacks teeth and money to reinstate places that have been damaged, although the worst impact has been through poor quality building, which the Duchy as land-lords have to bear most of the responsibility for. If the Trust had a good regular income, it would at least be possible to carry out most of the environmental work that needs doing. I think that income should come from a small landing fee charged to everybody arriving in Scilly. It could be used to employ local people to look after the islands.

Barry Philpott: We make small glass fibre day sailing boats, and dinghies. Sales are pretty much to local people and the market for me is mostly Tresco, because there are quite a lot of time-share visitors. I suppose the cheapest we make are the 7 ft dinghies for about £400. The most expensive for a basic boat is just under £6,000. We've just finished one that will run up to over £8,000 because of all the extras like bronze instead of galvanized fittings. Repairs are the mainstay of the business – wooden boats need a lot of money spent on them.

You can become very blinkered living here and it can be a real eye-opener going to the other boat-yards on the mainland and noticing the way they're marketing themselves. I have to make a conscious effort to look outside myself occasionally and try and keep in touch with new developments and materials. It's easy to lag behind.

Barry Philpott, thirty-four, came to Bryher in 1979 when his father was building the Hell Bay Hotel. He studied to be an environmental engineer and completed three years of the four year course before going to work in the catering trade. He began boatbuilding on Bryher with Keith Bennett, is married to Debbie, who runs a guest-house in their home, and they have two children.

THE FUND-RAISER

The person who was fund-raising on Bryher went to St Mary's and married, so rather than have nobody do it, I took it on. It's all for a good cause, so I don't mind at all. We live on the sea here, don't we? Visitors who know about the work the lifeboat does come into the cottage and have a look at what I'm selling. And anybody who is connected with lifeboats personally usually comes in just to say hello. It's nice to meet them. I think the furthest one that I definitely know of was from the Isle of Man.

My son John was born with salt water in his veins, no blood. He catches lobsters and crabs and I pick out the

Dorothy Pender, in her mid-seventies, is a Scillonian and lived on St Mary's as a child before coming to Bryher over fifty years ago. She is now a widow with four sons, and lives with John, the oldest. She has raised £25,000 for the lifeboat service in thirteen years.

125

crabs from the shells. I don't mind the picking though I do a bit of fussing, but it's alright really. I wouldn't live anywhere else. A week on the mainland and I'm fed up and glad to come home. All that rush and bustle, and all the cars.

In June this year we had a lovely buffet meal down in the Hell Bay Hotel and I was given a certificate ('The Committee of Management desire to record their warm thanks to Mrs Dorothy Pender for helping the lifeboat service, January 1993'). It really was a lovely evening.

I like having people come here, but when the season is getting on, then you're getting tired. We do in the winter what we can't do in the summer, painting and decorating and I like making shell pictures. There's never a dull moment. Never. But I wouldn't like to be doing nothing, I should go up the wall. I also look after my son, though he would say he looks after me.

THE BOATMAN

David Stedeford, forty-eight, was born and brought up on Bryher, and now runs the Bryher Boat Service with Ken Jenkins, with whom he's been in partnership for ten years. He is married to Kathy, who runs a holiday company, and they have two children.

The only break I've had away from the islands was five years in boarding school on the mainland and I couldn't wait to get home again. I did a couple of years with my father who was a flower farmer, but that wasn't really my scene and I started boating in a small way hiring out dinghies, running a few people to Tresco and Samson. It's grown from there.

We're very pleased with our new boat – she's steel, 60 ft long, 18 ft beam, and just a 2 ft 6 in draft which is exceptionally shallow for something this size. But she's purpose-built for the place and works very effectively. She can carry a hundred people with covered accommodation for three dozen seated, and fifty prepared to stand up.

We look after Bryher and Tresco exclusively, taking people to St Mary's six days a week, to St Martin's and St Agnes on alternate days. We also do circular trips to see birds and seals and are allowed to carry a dozen people an hour after sunset. The last scheduled boat from St Mary's is about 4.30 p.m., but we do special hire after that for late arrivals on the helicopter.

THE SHOPKEEPER

This was an almost derelict cottage when the Duchy offered it to us to set up a general store. It's very old, but not many post offices and shops have such a wonderful view over the water.

When we used to camp here on holiday long before we moved here, we could never get the things we wanted, so we try to stock a little bit of everything. People can go off the island from choice, but don't need to go chasing the essentials as we had to. We used to import the bread but it was often squashed or wet, or arrived late. Now I do all the baking – bread, fruit pies, pasties and cakes – I've got the day worked out to quite a fine art so I have something of everything ready by 9 a.m. In the peak of the season I start baking at quarter to four in the morning with rolls, pasties and fruit pies. Then I go into the fancy cakes. In the afternoon, I start the loaves and can make a maximum of twenty-four at a time. I carry on sometimes until midnight. In the peak of the summer I bake between 200 to 400 rolls a day, and in a really hectic week, can make up to 96 loaves a day.

At times like that I don't do much in the shop. Perhaps an hour a day. My husband, Ralph, and my daughter, Angela, do the till work but if Ralph is down at the quay meeting the launch for the supplies, it can be a bit of a nightmare at times. But mostly it works out. In the early part of the evening I help Angela with the evening meals in her guest-house. It keeps the adrenalin going, the challenge of it all.

June Bushell, fifty-four, and her husband, Ralph, came from Birmingham to run the general stores on Tresco before moving to Bryher to take over the post office and open a shop in 1985.

THE HOLIDAY ORGANIZER

We organize travel to the islands and whatever kind of accommodation people choose. Then we leave them to operate as individual travellers but if ever there is a problem, they can always get hold of me on the phone and, with the office at the end of our house, can pop in and say

Kathy Stedeford, fifty, worked as a hotel receptionist in Torquay and Falmouth before coming to Tresco in 1966 and, three years later, to Bryher where she has lived ever since. She is married to David, a partner in Bryher Boat Services, and they have a grown-up son and daughter. She has run the Isles of Scilly Inclusive Holidays for ten years.

'hello' if they want to. On a good year we bring in about nine hundred people.

I've got to try to be very impartial when advising people where to stay. It's pointless filling up the off-islands with people who don't actually want to be here, and I think some feel just that little bit more secure in St Mary's. When you talk to them on the phone, you sometimes pick up those you know would be happy here, and I don't think I've ever got it dreadfully wrong.

Some people hate leaving the security of their cars. If they have them, they feel they can go home if things don't work out. But the biggest hurdle some have to overcome is their anxiety about what there is to do in the evenings. I try and convince them they don't actually need any ready-made entertainment – people have forgotten that they can enjoy themselves with good company or a nice meal. And we've found that whichever off-island they come to first, they almost always return to that one. They go off on the boat in the morning to the other islands and feel it's like coming back home at the end of the day.

Kath Nicholls, fifty, a former nurse, came to Scilly as a child. Twenty-two years ago she and her husband, Jim, became managers of holiday cottages on Tresco. Now they run Vine Café, Kath doing the cooking and serving, Jim, a haulage contractor, the washing-up.

THE CAFÉ OWNER

I taught myself to cook and now make all my own bread, rolls and cakes like Swiss tarts, chocolate picnic slices, plum and almond torte, malt loaf, treacle tart, lemon and orange meringue, blackberry and raspberry pies. I make things that last for a couple of days and it's only scones that don't keep very well. If I have any left over, I usually give them to Rosalie the postmistress, who likes them toasted for breakfast. And I have to keep two or three back for my sparrows.

We close at the end of October and go to the mainland for about five or six weeks where I meet all the relatives, have a holiday and do my Christmas shopping. Then I usually go to Tresco and help tie their flowers.

THE MARKET GARDENERS

Becki Bridge, twenty-six, and Duncan Andrews, twenty-seven, came to work on Bryher in 1992. They met at a Devon agricultural college, where Duncan was studying agriculture, and Becki, food technology.

Duncan Andrews: We first took over about 12½ acres which were fallow or had daffodils, and have since got another 2½. Now 3 acres are down to mixed soft fruit, vegetables and salad crops and about 6 to daffodils and narcissi. We put strawberries in the first week we were here and have already been cropping some in our polythene tunnels. At the moment we're selling to Tresco, Bryher and St Mary's and the demand has been very encouraging. We have four pigs which use up waste food from the hotel, and hens are arriving at the end of the month.

Becki Bridge: We're doing things you don't tend to get over here like celeriac, Florence fennell, raddichio lettuces, garlic, melons. Strawberries are almost unheard of because they don't travel well. They only last a day after they've come over on the boat.

Duncan: We use as little inorganic fertilizer as possible and don't spray because, ethically, we don't want to. It's too early to tell if it's all going to work – we'll have to get at least a year behind us to know.

Becki: We've now got two tunnels and a little greenhouse for propagation. It would be nice to have a larger one, but you can't get them insured because of the gales. You feel so powerless against the wind and the only thing you can do is put up shelters and new hedging which you have to wait to get established. But we have a fairly large house and one self-contained end is let for holidays. Without that income it would be very hard to survive over here. We wouldn't have come back, in fact, if we hadn't had that security.

ST AGNES

St Agnes, 2 miles long by 1 mile across with a population of about sixty-two, is the most south-westerly community in Britain. It has rocky shores, sandy coves, butterflies and wild flowers on the downland, and is linked at low tide to the tiny island of Gugh, which has two houses and the Old Man of Gugh, an ancient stone probably dating from the Bronze Age.

There are seven farms, two cafés, a pub, a post office and general stores, a church built in 1887, the third on the same site, a bulb shop, guest-houses, self-catering cottages, and a camp site. Model shipwright Danny Hick makes yachts and pilot gigs which are sold all over the world.

A squat lighthouse, erected in 1680 and now privately owned, stands over a cluster of cottages built for the original lighthouse keepers and their families. There's a primary school with eight children, and Troy Town Maze, a labyrinth of pebbles thought to have been made by a lighthouse keeper in 1729, but which may be much older. At Beady Pool you can sometimes still find beads in the sand from a Dutch ship wrecked here in the seventeenth century.

In winter the rectangular fields are full of daffodils, in summer dark pink gladioli, known as Whistling Jacks. Throughout most of the year, bird-watchers make their way to The Pool for the great variety of species to be found here.

THE BULB SHOP OWNERS

Adrian, forty-three, and Mandy Pearce, forty-two, are Scillonians: Mandy's family have been on St Agnes for about three hundred years, Adrian came from St Mary's. When they were first married they worked in London and Cornwall before moving back to Scilly in 1973, and taking over the farm in 1980. They have two children. Their work includes sending flowers to the mainland markets, flowers by post, and selling bulbs, plants and home-made candles in The Bulb Shop.

Adrian: We always knew we were going to come back and flower farm here. We love Scilly. We farm about 10 acres, 5 of which are in bulbs, predominantly the Tazetta varieties, like *Soleil d'Or* and the Paper Whites. It's not as good as it used to be but we've survived because we've managed to diversify.

Mandy: We have holiday lets which keep us going and The Bulb Shop makes money out of the farm. The decision to diversify was a conscious one not to go on as we were – flowers weren't making money any more and we didn't particularly want to be spending all our winters with Adrian bent over picking flowers and me sitting here tying them. Someone on the island said you can always tell a flower tier because their eyes are glazed. It *is* dull and boring and the shop is much more interesting.

Our two children go to school here and with only eight in all, they've got practically one-to-one teaching. The school is equipped with computers as well as anywhere else. They have the challenge of going to school on St Mary's when they're eleven and becoming weekly boarders. They're a bit anxious about it, but there's a lot of liaising between the two schools, so they are aware of what is going to happen.

I'd give them the same advice as my mother gave me. She said, 'Don't come back. You'll spend all your life working and worrying about whether you're going to have enough money to see you through next year.' And, of course, it's quite true, you do worry. You have a gale when you've got a good crop of flowers in the fields and you can lose the next £400 you're counting on. We've always been under-capitalized, and if we hadn't had the farm from my parents, we wouldn't have been able to cope at all. There's recently been a family who've been bankrupted by moving here and trying to farm, and I think the same would probably have happened to us in all honesty.

THE SHOPKEEPER AND POSTMISTRESS

When we took the shop over it was probably about a third the size it is now. There was no help-yourself and a much lower annual turnover. We have a good turnover per capita through the winter, too, but with a population of about eighty we don't open the same number of hours. It's just me here, and John does all the building construction. We don't run out of things very often – the launch with provisions nearly always gets through. It can come in a Force 9 though we do get problems sometimes when our supplies disappear to another island by mistake, but we usually manage to find them.

I wouldn't like to live on any of the other islands. You have to find the one that suits you. For me, St Agnes is very special, we think it's the one most like Scilly used to be,

Penny Hale, fifty-one, a former teacher, came to Scilly on holiday for ten years before deciding to live here. She is married to John, whom she met on the island, and they now run the only shop on St Agnes.

133

and the seven flower farms create an important part of its atmosphere in that it's not just geared to tourism. Life here in the winter goes on very much as it does the rest of the year except there aren't so many visitors around, though we might have a few staying on a long let, writing a book or painting.

Although we took the shop over from Don, who was an islander, we weren't in competition with any other islander who wanted it. I think all the services on St Agnes are run by outsiders and that's because Scillonians don't particularly want to have the shop or the pub or the cafés. They're happy farming and fishing. If you come here, you're given a terrific welcome and if you don't get on with the islanders, it's down to you. There's no resentment at all.

Activities? Last year I joined the Choral Society, but it's very difficult to get across to St Mary's for rehearsals in the evening, almost impossible unless you have your own boat. At the moment, cricket is the thing – we haven't got the tennis court going this year. Most reading is done through our paperbacks and we're quite renowned for them. My mail order is about £700, wholesale price, a month in the peak season – we put through an order every week for about thirty or forty books. If someone gives us an order on a Monday, I can have the book by Wednesday.

THE CAMP SITE PROPRIETOR

I was a bit apprehensive coming to live here – I knew it was just not like anywhere else. I think if you don't make it here, you feel almost a failure. Not always, of course. It doesn't suit everyone, but I felt that. The farm is about 15 acres, and we have three self-catering lets as well as the camp site. It had been going for ten years before we came, but was very basic – two thunder boxes and a tank of water if you were lucky, which suited people fine in those days, but their expectations have increased. One of our first projects was to put up a toilet block, with showers, hot water, a wash-room and drying facilities. We kept it simple because that's what people really like here. But there was

Sue Hicks, forty, a former teacher, comes from mainland Cornwall. She married Tim, a Scillonian from St Agnes, at that time in the Royal Navy, whose brother took over the family farm. When another farm became available ten years ago, Sue and Tim moved back to run it and the camp site.

nearly a revolution because in our plans we included what we called a games room. It had a table tennis table and somewhere to shelter if the weather was bad. But the campers at the time had visions of space invaders, which wouldn't be St Agnes at all.

We had to improve the water supply – it was all rain water – and get a deep bore hole. We got a water diviner to come over, and he worked on the principle of no water, no pay, which was a good deal. Once we said we'd do it, quite a few other people said, 'Well, can we have one too?' I won't say water is plentiful now, but it's nothing like as bad as it was before.

When campers come, they walk from the boat, but we bring their luggage up on the tractor. When the sun is shining, they can't quite believe it, they are so close to the sea – the site is immediately above the shore line. They get most of their supplies from the local shop and we supply fresh milk, dairy produce and potatoes. I make the cream, butter and yoghurt. It's hard work, but I enjoy it and people seem to like it. I'm usually cleared by mid-morning and then I often have paperwork to do. I've had a computer for about eighteen months and print my own booking forms and information sheets – I also act as a sort of clearing house on the island for vacancies for the people with self-catering and B&B accommodation.

Some of the jobs are monotonous in themselves, but because they're so different, no two days are alike. I go weeks before getting as far as St Mary's, which doesn't bother me at all. Do I miss anything? Marks and Sparks [laughs], woodlands and streams. We haven't got any streams here.

Fred Smith, sixty-three, was the last person to be born on St Agnes. He went to Truro School, joined the RAF but was grounded because of migraines, worked with a building company, and opened an estate agency in Somerset. After being away from Scilly for about thirty years, he returned eleven years ago. He was a local councillor for four years, and is married to Sheila, a councillor in her second term. He has his own boat, and holiday cottages to let.

THE PIANIST

We had a very good schoolteacher here on St Agnes – Miss Tiddy – and she taught me to play the piano. This is hers, a Steinway, and there aren't many of those in Scilly. I play by ear and with music, but mainly by ear, because it saves carrying music around. I do sing-along stuff basically but have played at the St Martin's Hotel and The Island Hotel on Tresco which is a bit different to playing in a pub where you can get people to sing.

The Turks Head here is one of the best pubs in the islands. There's a nice atmosphere and lovely food, and of course, all the visitors know me and say, 'You going down to the pub tonight?' Most people like a sing-song and live music even if they don't join in. The old songs are the ones they like best – 'Daisy', 'My Old Man Says Follow the Band' – we play anything. The French people come in and they want 'Sur le Pont d'Avignon', and the Dutch have some risque ones that I don't know the words for. We get people dancing occasionally, a few wild French can-cans and hokey-kokeys.

I suppose, on reflection, playing the piano is the only thing I can do without too much effort. If I'd put more into it, I might have done something with it, but there's a tremendous amount of competition, isn't there?

THE ISLANDER

Dorothy Barker, sixty-five, was born on St Agnes, and has lived here all her life. She is married to Maurice, an electrician who came with his parents from Derbyshire in 1948 to live on Gugh. Her grandfather and father coxed *The Gypsy* pilot boat.

I can remember the time when we had candles and oil lamps, and when Maurice and I came to this house in 1956, we had an old wind generator out in the back garden. It used to make a terrible row. It was alright when there was a gale blowing, there was plenty of force, but when there wasn't much wind, the light used to go up and down.

Television has changed things. We don't seem to get together in the evenings as we used to do. We had social evenings up at the school every Saturday and whist drives. We used to alternate, one week whist drive, the following Saturday a social evening, and everybody was asked to make a plate of cakes. We used to have a dance first, then an interval, then refreshments, and then they'd play games and more dancing. Eddie Hicks used to play the piano, his brother, Lewis, the violin, and our old teacher, Miss Tiddy, would come in and play the piano. I've got this old photograph of her standing by the school gate with skirts down to her ankles, a big felt hat and a walking stick.

THE FLOWER FARMER

I came straight back from secondary school on St Mary's – this is such a different type of farming that there's really no agricultural college that would teach you what is needed. I've been in it now for twenty-two years and I'm still learning. The farm – just narcissus, Tazetta, multi-headed sweet-scented ones – has been in the family for generations. The house is about five hundred years old and for all we know, it could have been built by my relations. It leaks and is damp, like a nice old house should be. Unfortunately flower farming is a business where we get what other people will pay us. I go country-wide, mostly to the southern markets, and send between 1,200 and 1,500 boxes a year, 500 to 600 flowers in a box. They're packed up, chilled, sent off on the inter-island launch to Penzance and then on to lorries to wherever I wish them to go. On St Agnes we're basically all independent. There is a co-operative marketing group on St Mary's, Mainland Marketing, who do a lot of direct selling but I like to make my own contacts and know who I'm dealing with.

Mike Hicks, thirty-seven, is a flower farmer, an auxiliary coastguard, keeps cows and bees, and is making a study of island moths. He is married to Christine and they have three children.

I've got a couple of cows that supply our own milk and a couple of other houses on the island. We get about 6 to 7 gallons a day – it's full-bodied milk, unpasteurized. We tell people it is, and if they accept that, they can have it. Of course, it's perfectly good for you because it's been drunk for generations. With a small herd, it's not intense which is where the trouble starts and disease is passed on. Visitors say, 'Oh how good to be able to taste a pint of real milk again.' I've also got some chickens – one of the cafés has eggs from us and the shop takes them in the winter.

We have about 14 acres, an average sort of size for an off-island farm. We're so limited for land we can't rest it, we're always recycling and planting bulbs back in within twelve months of lifting them.

We've recently bought over a hundred and fifty new varieties of bulbs that were bred specifically for the islands and a group of growers are carrying on experimental work with them on St Mary's. Many chemicals for diseases that get into bulbs have been banned through, so far as I can tell, mis-use on the mainland, and we suffer the consequences over here. At present there's a daffodil fly which we used to treat with Aldrin in the ground and I've seen no adverse affects on our crop or wild life whatsoever, even though it's been used here for fifty years. However, it's been banned on the mainland and they've taken it off the market. Now there are no recommended chemicals for use against this particular fly. The islands would be an ideal place to do a biological control study, but being a small industry, government won't put any research into funding it.

A couple of years ago I started bees – the flowers are there, so we might as well reap the harvest from them. Last year I did particularly well and managed to take off 150 lb of honey. We sell it through the local shop or other islanders buy it for Christmas presents. The bees even go across the water to Gugh where there's a lot of heather growing on the rough ground, and they really do fly in a bee line – I saw them all going through this same little gap in the trees to get back to the hives.

Apart from trying to sell some of our produce to the tourist trade, we basically make our living solely from the farm. That's very unusual now. Talk to anyone, particularly after the last bad flower season, and they say, 'Well, at least we've got the holiday lets to make a living from', and I say I haven't, and they say, 'How come you're still smiling?' It's hard work I suppose, just grafting away, trying to produce the best quality, rather than quantity, and hope one gets that bit extra for it.

I always thought I'd live here. I haven't been off the island for two and a half years and it wouldn't worry me if I didn't go off for another two and a half. I like the thought of being cut off! If it's too rough for the *Scillonian* or the cargo boat, or it's foggy and the helicopter and Skybus can't fly, you hear on the news that Scilly is cut off from the mainland. We're just waiting for the day when they say the mainland is cut off from Scilly.

INDEX